EXPERIENCING AMERICAN HOUSES

EXPERIENCING AMERICAN HOUSES

Understanding How Domestic Architecture Works

ELIZABETH COLLINS CROMLEY

Vernacular Architecture Studies
Alison K. Hoagland, Series Editor

THE UNIVERSITY OF TENNESSEE PRESS / KNOXVILLE

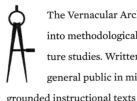

The Vernacular Architecture Studies series provides focused investigations into methodological and theoretical issues in the field of vernacular architecture studies. Written by experts in the field with the student, practitioner, and general public in mind, the series will comprise handbooks and historically grounded instructional texts that embody the very latest research from a burgeoning discipline in an accessible, practical form.

Copyright © 2022 by The University of Tennessee Press / Knoxville.
All Rights Reserved. Manufactured in the United States of America.
First Edition.

Library of Congress Cataloging-in-Publication Data

Names: Cromley, Elizabeth C., author.

Title: Experiencing American houses : understanding how domestic architecture works / Elizabeth Collins Cromley.

Description: First edition. | Knoxville : The University of Tennessee Press, [2022] | Series: Vernacular architecture studies | Includes bibliographical references and index. | Summary: "This book encourages readers to think creatively about buildings in terms of their function and how these functions have changed over time in American history. The work presents material culture as lived experience and is designed to expand the encounter with material culture to look beyond house styles to how various household spaces (kitchens, living rooms, bedrooms, etc.) have been seen and felt in American life. This volume is the third in a series, Vernacular Architecture Studies, publishing introductory texts on aspects of material culture, often aimed at non-specialists"—Provided by publisher.

Identifiers: LCCN 2021042880 (print) | LCCN 2021042881 (ebook) | ISBN 9781621904410 (paperback) | ISBN 9781621904427 (kindle edition) | ISBN 9781621904434 (adobe pdf)

Subjects: LCSH: Architecture, Domestic—Social aspects—United States. | Domestic space—United States. | Vernacular architecture—United States. | Architecture and society—United States.

Classification: LCC NA7205 .C755 2022 (print) | LCC NA7205 (ebook) | DDC 728.0973—dc23

LC record available at https://lccn.loc.gov/2021042880

LC ebook record available at https://lccn.loc.gov/2021042881

CONTENTS

Foreword   xi
  Alison K. Hoagland
Acknowledgments   xiii
Introduction   xv

1 | Spaces for Cooking   1

2 | Socializing: Parlor, Living Room, Family Room,
    Living-Kitchen   31

3 | Spaces for Eating   51

4 | Sleeping, Health, and Privacy   71

5 | Circulation, or Getting from Here to There   105

6 | Storage   129

7 | Conclusion   151

Notes   157
For Further Reading   175
Index   183

ILLUSTRATIONS

Fig. 1. Freestanding Brick Kitchen, Brush-Everard House, Colonial Williamsburg   3

Fig. 2. Plan of the Boardman House   5

Fig. 3a. Dairy, Winslow House, Marshfield, Massachusetts, and **Fig. 3b.** Dairy Building, Eyre Hall, Eastern Shore of Maryland, c. 1800   6

Fig. 4. Three Doors in the Kitchen of the 1786 Burtch-Udall Homestead, Queechee, Vermont   7

Fig. 5. Root Cellar, Butte, Montana   8

Fig. 6. Tripod at the Virginia Mansion, Stratford   10

Fig. 7. Drawing of Progression of Cooking at the Tobias Walker Farm, Kennebunk, Maine   11

Fig. 8. Kitchen and Rear Ell, 1807 Rundlett-May House in Portsmouth, New Hampshire   13

Fig. 9. Plan of the 1860 Gibson House, Boston   14

Fig. 10. The Magee Grand Range of 1894   16

Fig. 11. Vaux and Radford's Tenement Apartment   17

Fig. 12. Plan for Van Dyck House, New Jersey, Including Butler's Pantries   20

Fig. 13. Plan of Isabel Bevier's Inexpensive Suburban Home, 1912   21

Fig. 14. Advertisement for an Ice-Box, c. 1897   22

Fig. 15. Drawing of the Kohl Sisters' Homesteading Shack, c. 1908   24

Fig. 16. A 1927 Electric Refrigerator   26

Fig. 17. Keene's Design for an Early Twentieth-Century Kitchen   27

Fig. 18. Sears Modern Kitchen, 1951   28

Fig. 19. Veggli House at Old World Wisconsin, 1840s   32

Fig. 20. Overview of Shirley Plantation in Virginia   33

Fig. 21. Plan of Calvert Vaux   35

Fig. 22. Gleason's "Parlor View in a New York Dwelling," 1859   36

Fig. 23. Plan of the Boyce House, Chicago   37

Fig. 24. Plan of a Cheap Flat for the Working Poor, 1874   39

Fig. 25. Carved Rosewood Chair and Later Craftsman-Style Unornamented Oak Chair   41

Fig. 26. Plan of the Kentucky Bungalow, by the Aladdin Co., 1919   42

Fig. 27. Armstrong Tile Advertisement Featuring

Midcentury Rec Room   45

Fig. 28. Barry Wills Open Plan, 1955   46

Fig. 29. Bird's-Eye View of Almon Fordyce Living Kitchen, 1945   47

Fig. 30. Spruce Lake Model House from Timberhaven Log

and Timber Homes Brochure   49

Fig. 31. Drawing of Expansion of Randolph Family's Virginia House,

Tuckahoe, 1740   53

Fig. 32. Nature Themes in Dining Room   57

Fig. 33. Plan of the 1883 Central Park Apartments   58

Fig. 34. A Maid Serves Nine, 1888   59

Fig. 35a. Floor Plan of the Ansonia Apartment-Hotel and

Fig. 35b. Detail of its Kitchenless Apartments, New York, 1907   60

Fig. 36. Drawing of Combination Living Room

and Dining Room, 1927   62

Fig. 37. House Plan Featuring Built-in Nook by Architect

Charles E. White, 1923   63

Fig. 38. Modest Dwelling in Greenbelt, Maryland, 1939   63

Fig. 39. A Counter with Stools at the Z-Bar Ranch,

Washington, Kansas   64

Fig. 40. Plan of an Inexpensive House Combining Dining

and Kitchen Areas, 1920s   66

Fig. 41. Plan of Middle-Class House by Pearce Developers of Buffalo,

New York, 1959   68

Fig. 42. Tip-Up Bedstead, Common in Seventeeth

and Eighteenth Centuries   73

Fig. 43. Fine Eighteenth-Century Bedstead That Belonged

to John Bartram   73

Fig. 44. Plan of James Cleaves House, Winchester, Massachusetts   75

Fig. 45. Period Drawing of One-Room Frontier Houses in

Salt Lake City in 1850   77

Fig. 46. Wyollah Slave Cottage, Adams County, Mississippi   78

Fig. 47. Tenement Apartment Plans for Two Units Per Floor,

New York before 1879   80

Fig. 48. Replica Slave House at Mount Vernon in Virginia   81

Fig. 49. Small Servant's Room at Biltmore Estate, Asheville,

North Carolina   81

Fig. 50. Drawing of a Mother Tucking Her Child into Bed,
Featuring Portable Bathtub, 1889   83

Fig. 51a. Common Bedroom Pitcher and Basin and **Fig. 51b.**
Advertisement for Patent "Combination Bathtub," 1924   83

Fig. 52. Advertisement for Universal Commode Cabinet, 1884   84

Fig. 53a. Privy at Nineteenth-Century Workers' Housing, Batsto,
New Jersey, and **Fig. 53b.** Poplar Hill, Maryland, Privy   85

Fig. 54a. Modern Bathroom with Toilet, Sink, and Bathtub, and
Fig. 54b. Upper-Class Bathroom with Decorative Features, 1903   86

Fig. 55a. Drawing of Tip-Up Bed, 1891, and **Fig. 55b.** Hinged
"Door Beds" White Efficiency Apartment   88

Fig. 56a. Detail of Watrous House, Mora County, New Mexico,
and **Fig. 56b.** The Watrous House Plan   90

Fig. 57. Destrehan Plantation, Featuring Freestanding Garçonnières   91

Fig. 58. Plan of a One-Floor Apartment at 78 Irving Place, 1901   92

Fig. 59. Wooden Bed in the Bedroom of A. J. Miller House,
Augusta County, Virginia   94

Fig. 60a and **Fig. 60b.** Two Patent Devices to Bring Fresh Air
to Bedrooms   95

Fig. 61. Oliver Smith Design for a Farmhouse, 1854   96

Fig. 62. Plan for Second-Story Master Suite, 1916   100

Fig. 63. Front Door, Jackson House, Portsmouth, New Hampshire,
Built in the 1660s   106

Fig. 64a. Front Door, John Paul Jones House, Portsmouth, New
Hampshire, Built 1758, and **Fig. 64b.** Twentieth-Century Public
Housing, Alexandria, Virginia   107

Fig. 65a. Dining-Room Door at Poplar Hill in Clinton, Maryland,
and **Fig. 65b.** Dining-Room Doorway for Servants   108

Fig. 66. Farnsworth House Glass Door, Plano, Illinois, 1950   109

Fig. 67. Two Levels of Front Doors on a House, Friendship,
Maine, Built c. 2000   110

Fig. 68. Center-Hall Plan, Warner House, Portsmouth,
New Hampshire, c. 1720   112

Fig. 69. Servants' Stair View, Bellamy House, Wilmington,
North Carolina, Built c. 1860   113

Fig. 70. Hall Stand, Coolmore Plantation, North Carolina   114

Fig. 71. Improved Dwellings Association Design for Tenements
in New York, 1889   116

Fig. 72. Plan for Multiple Halls, Berkshire Apartments, 1880s   117

Fig. 73. Design for Multiple Stair Landings, 1878   119

Fig. 74. Small House Plan Using Bathroom as Circulation   123

Fig. 75. Plan for Double- or Two-Family House,
Buffalo, New York, c. 1905   125

Fig. 76. Modern Open Plan for House 6, Architect V. Furno
and J. Harrison, 1948   126

Fig. 77. Vaulted Cellar at Belair in Maryland,
Built Eighteenth Century   130

Fig. 78. Drawing of Cellar, Christian Ley House,
Tulpehocken, Pennsylvania, c. 1750   131

Fig. 79. Plan for Ice Room, Glessner House, Chicago, 1887   132

Fig. 80a and **Fig. 80b.** Eighteenth-Century China Closet,
Maple Hill Farm, Norwich, Vermont   134

Fig. 81. Plan for Two-Pantry House, Evanston, Illinois, 1891   135

Fig. 82. Drawing of "A Well-arranged Pantry," 1884   136

Fig. 83. Nineteenth-Century Pantry, Quincy, Illiniois, Built 1888   136

Fig. 84. Sears Roebuck Kitchen, 1940s   138

Fig. 85. Plan for Asher Benjamin Design, 1806   140

Fig. 86. Plan Featuring Closets, Architect Calvert Vaux, 1857   142

Fig. 87a. Movable Closet with Daytime Pictures,
and **Fig. 87b.** Closet with Nighttime Storage   143

Fig. 88. Lydia Ray Balderston's 1928 House Design Featuring
Shoe Storage Closet   144

Fig. 89. Outdoor Storage in Backyard, Galesville, Virginia   147

Fig. 90. Attached Garages, Belair Subdivision, Bowie, Maryland,
Built c. 1961   148

FOREWORD

Experiencing American Houses takes a fresh approach to understanding and analyzing historic houses. Rather than focusing on how these dwellings *look*, this book examines how dwellings *function*. The ways people use houses are familiar to all of us—eating, sleeping, cooking, socializing, storing our stuff, and so on. The analysis that Elizabeth Collins Cromley brings to this knowledge is to examine how those functions are expressed in architecture. Throughout time, while uses stay largely the same, the architecture changes, suggesting that the house displays meanings as much as it accommodates functions. When residents or guests experience a house, they are receiving these meanings as much as they are utilizing its practical, physical attributes.

Cromley sets an essential context for understanding how the broad purposes, or functions, of American domestic architecture evolve through time, in different regions of the country, and across class. Something as universal as a bedroom or a kitchen is shown to be subject to complex changes and understandings in different eras or places, or when intended for different social classes. While this book is directed at students, it will also become a necessary text for anyone who looks at historical houses in an analytical framework. Homeowners, too, should find this book useful in challenging their basic assumptions about their own houses.

Experiencing American Houses is the third volume in the Vernacular Architecture Studies series, a venture of the Vernacular Architecture Forum and the University of Tennessee Press. Along with Thomas Carter, Cromley co-authored the first volume in the series, *Invitation to Vernacular Architecture: A Guide to the Study of Ordinary Buildings and Landscapes*. Thomas C. Hubka wrote the second, *Houses Without Names: Architectural Nomenclature and the Classification of America's Common Houses*. Together, these three books offer ways of understanding the common buildings that surround us. While ordinary houses or barns or stores may not grab our attention at first glance, these buildings make up the built landscape and have the capacity to tell us about how we lived and who we are. The volumes in this series show us how to approach and analyze this built landscape.

Founded in 1980, the Vernacular Architecture Forum is a group of scholars and practitioners who study the built landscape with an eye toward why buildings have taken the shape they have, how they have changed over time, and what meanings they have held. The group has an annual meeting that focuses on exploring and understanding the buildings and landscapes of the local region, while also offering academic papers. Our members' work ranges widely, across North America and beyond, from the seventeenth century to the present, from minimal dwellings to imposing churches. The Vernacular Architecture Studies series is intended to explain our approach to the built environment. *Experiencing American Houses* takes just one focus of our efforts—the house—and introduces the reader to the myriad ways in which it can be understood.

Alison K. Hoagland
Series Editor, Vernacular Architecture Studies

ACKNOWLEDGMENTS

My thinking about how people use spaces has been encouraged and supported by the members of the Vernacular Architecture Forum, a national organization founded in 1980 to lead the study of ordinary buildings. VAF-organized study trips to forty-six of the contiguous states have given me opportunities to visit many of the buildings under discussion and to photograph them. Reading the research materials provided to attendees at these meetings is like taking a course in each region's architecture and landscapes.

I credit the study of vernacular (or ordinary) architecture with adding to the questions that traditional architectural historians used to ask. We consider a building's style or aesthetic, its materials, and who designed or built it; but then we ask, how has it changed over time? How have its residents used its spaces and how have they changed those uses? How has the building been adapted to suit climate or ethnic demands? How does the building convey some of the inhabitants' values? The journal *Buildings and Landscapes* and its predecessor *Perspectives in Vernacular Architecture* have published research by VAF members including myself, keeping this field of study lively and giving all of us the opportunity to be lifelong learners.

My research over the years has been supported by many institutions. I am especially grateful to The Winterthur Library and Museum (residency programs for scholars), the Radcliffe Institute for Advanced Study (Berkshire Fellowship), Northeastern University (research grants to faculty; provost's grants for student researchers), and for grants from the National Endowment for the Humanities (Fellowships for College Teachers). Librarians at the New York Public Library, the Boston Public Library, Winterthur Library, Chicago Historical Society, Schlessinger Library, and Northeastern University Library have always been ready to help. I thank Mary Hughes at Northeastern for invaluable help with illustrations.

I want to thank The University of Tennessee Press for providing me with very helpful comments from anonymous readers. My thanks especially to Alison K. Hoagland for her heading the VAF Book Series committee, which works with The University of Tennessee Press to select new books on vernacular architecture topics, and for encouraging and guiding the completion of this book.

I want to thank The University of Tennessee Press for providing me with very helpful comments from anonymous readers. My thanks especially to Alison K. Hoagland for her heading the VAF Book Series committee, which works with The University of Tennessee Press to select new books on vernacular architecture topics, and for encouraging and guiding the completion of this book.

INTRODUCTION

We are all familiar with the functional spaces we expect to find inside typical American dwellings—specific locations assigned to cooking, to eating, to socializing, to sleeping, to storage, and some paths of movement to get us through these spaces and from the outside to the inside. The dwellings we live in or visit may take the form of freestanding houses, mobile homes, two-family duplexes or triple-deckers, urban row-house types, apartments in high- or low-rise buildings containing multiple dwelling units—or even spaces for current living repurposed from former factories, churches, or schools. But whatever the exterior form or dwelling type, we would expect to find spaces within the walls that support very similar functions. We also expect certain kinds of equipment and furnishings to be proper to each of these spaces—for example, beds in bedrooms, sinks in kitchens and bathrooms.

Such functional spaces and "correct" furnishings are not the rule, however, when we look at how the interiors of houses have been used historically. Imagine it is the year 1840. You are visiting a friend and he invites you to take a look at his newly built dining room addition. You see a dining table, benches, and a chair, but also a bed off to the side, several hoes and shovels in the corner, bunches of herbs hung up to dry from the ceiling beams, and a sack of flour near the door. These furnishings are far from the ones we would find in twenty-first-century urban or rural dining spaces, but not uncommon in houses built during the era of Midwestern homesteading in the mid- and late nineteenth century.

This book helps you understand how the rooms you are now looking at represent one of numerous ways that people have created historically changing places to cook, sleep, socialize, eat, walk around, or store goods within their dwellings. What sorts of people would have had dining rooms in their houses in 1810—or in 2010? Where would families eat their meals if they didn't have a dining room? When you visit a historic house museum and see its dining room, or see the dining-room of your friends down the street, this book will give you a context in which to place the dining activity in the history of house-inhabiting. Likewise, the book explores the other common functions of the house. Where did people sleep in various historical periods and geographical regions? Where did they manage cooking?

What arrangements did they make for sociability—in special rooms like parlors, or in spaces combined with a mix of domestic activities? How did people store their possessions in houses? The book will provide a historic context for the way each of these familiar domestic functions has evolved.[1]

This book invites ways to think about how an American house functions for the people who live in it—in the past or currently—but I will limit my examination to houses built by European, African, Asian, and other immigrants. Native American dwellings are not included here. The time period in the book runs from the seventeenth century to the turn of the present century. The chapters trace chronological developments, but readers should expect to find overlaps and interleavings among the chapters. Dwellings respond to the number of people comprising the household, which may be small or large or change from large to small with the resident family's own decades. Regional and climate differences affect how closed or open a dwelling will be and whether its functions can be located outdoors or in. The social class and income of the residents shape their use of spaces. Each variable had its own standards for how a dwelling should be lived in as dwellers accommodated new inventions, building materials, manners, or family relations. It is satisfying to learn the details of architectural styles when contemplating how dwellings look, and several books are available to help identify the various historic styles used in American architecture, but if one is to live in a house, its style is mainly just an envelope for the life the house will contain.[2]

I want to shift attention away from the style of houses and their aesthetic properties towards how inhabitants have actually used houses. The book focuses on *experiencing* American houses and how houses *work*. We can find out something about how dwellers experienced their rooms from letters, diaries, autobiographies and records such as travelers' accounts and photographs. Sometimes fiction also gives glimpses of people's experience of their houses. When I ask how the house works, I focus on the architectural spaces—typically rooms—that mark out where specific activities should happen.[3] How does the architecture support the functions or convey the meanings that dwellers want, and secure spaces that meet their (sometimes conflicting) needs? These architectural frameworks and people's accounts of their experiences using them give us a general sense of the way houses have met domestic desires for meaningful, functional spaces over the decades. At the same time, I am always curious as to how rooms were used contrary to their official purposes, in the expectation that spaces often support new uses if their users want to be inventive.

Sorting the complexity of life in a house into a few themes will make this exploration manageable. Everyone needs to prepare food and eat somewhere; entertain or just sit and relax somewhere; sleep and care for the body's needs somewhere in or near the house; move through the house from outdoors to in, down to up, and front to back; and store supplies and possessions when they aren't in use. The book's chapters will focus on these themes: "Spaces for Cooking," "Socializing: Parlor, Living Room, Family Room, Living-Kitchen," "Spaces for Eating," "Sleeping, Health, and Privacy," "Circulation, or Getting from Here to There," and "Storage." A seventh chapter, "Conclusions," suggests some thoughts about how several issues cut across these chapter topics and invites readers to generate their own questions. Finally, a bibliography suggests further readings.

If you were to visit the first house type commonly built in the seventeenth century, it would have one room, and the main feature of its one room would be a fireplace built for cooking. This is why I begin with cooking space. Next, we consider space for socializing in two chapters—rooms organized specifically for visiting and entertaining, and rooms designed for socializing over meals served to family or guests. The next chapter considers how and where people slept, cleaned themselves, and established privacy. Paths of movement around the house allow boundaries to be respected among the several functions, separating or blending different realms of experience inside the house. Finally dwelling in comfort requires storing goods of all sorts—from food to clothes to cars—in a hole in the ground, a closet, or a garage.

I follow how rooms were named as broad indications of changes in use over the decades. The shifting names assigned to different rooms can be traced in period inventories, in letters and diaries, in the labels on published plans, and in magazine articles and books giving advice to home-dwellers. One doesn't know for certain if the actual inhabitants of a house always called their rooms by the names in these sources, but it is the best evidence we have. Visual evidence in these pages will help you see how and when changes took place. The illustrations include views of interiors—photographs and drawings—as well as house plans. Plans may not be as entertaining to look at but they tell us a lot about where specific rooms were located in houses, what these rooms were called, how different functions were separated or joined, and how one could move around the house through rooms, doors, corridors, and stairs.

The range of classes and incomes served by American houses is endlessly varied; we will include examples of houses lived in or designed for rich and poor, native-born and foreign-born inhabitants, located in cities, suburbs, and rural settings. I do use the terms "working class" or "middle class," knowing that these do not designate specific income levels but instead are terms that allowed people to locate themselves in contrast to the classes they perceived to compete with them for cultural space. The United States is vast, but in the course of this book we will include examples of houses in many states. They respond to widely differing climates and regional building traditions. The historical time span of the book from the 1600s to 2000 includes examples of houses typically thought of as "historical" as well as more modern ones, which are also historical albeit of a more recent sort.

I hope that readers will be surprised by the variety of ways that American houses have been used and understood. Our normal practices of cooking in kitchens or sleeping in bedrooms turn out to be recent; historical records show us many other places to sleep in a house or cook outside of the kitchens we now inhabit. When we consider the many historical alternatives in using the spaces of a house and its nearby landscape, we may emerge grateful for the modern, well-defined functions the typical house supports. But this encounter may also help us imagine how our daily-life architecture could take on innovative spatial forms or invite different activities in the future.

EXPERIENCING AMERICAN HOUSES

1

SPACES FOR COOKING

American houses and their home grounds have, since the first European settlements, included spaces for preparing food. You might expect that a chapter about cooking would start with identifying all the components of a kitchen, but kitchens as organized sites for cooking do not appear in houses for a couple of centuries after the first settlers arranged to cook in or near their houses. What we will see instead is householders distributing places for food preservation, storage, and preparation around the homesite, only gathering them into one rationalized kitchen by the turn of the twentieth century.

Within New England or Chesapeake houses of the seventeenth century, the cooking space was initially a fire built on the earthen floor. Smoke from the fire rose through a smoke-hole in the roof, framed in wood. In warmer climates early houses had outdoor kettles hung over a fire where stews braised. As masonry materials became available, colonists built large fireplaces—the principal or only hearth on which they laid their cooking fire—in the main, or only, room which they typically called the hall. Cooking fireplaces, high and wide, were outfitted with cranes, spits, and other iron tools to aid in cooking. The fireplace often had an oven built into the back, side, or front masonry wall for baking. Centuries later we now call this space a kitchen, and we think of it as a place where appliances are concentrated, cooking equipment stored, and even if we don't cook much, as a place with a sink, stove or microwave, and refrigerator.[1]

Similarly the purposeful shaping of the landscape around dwellings also responded to the demand for food. As colonists cleared land for their houses and harvested timber from forested regions, they began cultivating gardens to provide for family nourishment and saved pieces of wood to make cooking fires. In southern colonies dedicated to large plantations of single crops, residents also planted food gardens for their own needs.

Decorative landscaping and ornamental garden beds would follow in the eighteenth century, but the first landscape interventions around the New World colonies' houses were developed to satisfy the need for food. By 1700 the taste for function-specific, food-related rooms had spread along the Eastern Seaboard. In New England, such rooms tended to find their places within the bounds of the house, but in more forgiving climates and under different social circumstances, function-specific outbuildings were constructed adjacent to houses.

The overall direction of this chapter is a story of consolidation and merging. At first huge fireplaces contained cooking, either within the main house or in food-related outbuildings. When cooking facilities consolidated around 1800, formerly dispersed sites' functions were moved into house interiors and concentrated in kitchens. Cooking often moved toward the rear of houses, whose backs collected work spaces while their fronts preserved politeness. Cooking spaces responded to efficiency experts, leading to small and super-organized kitchens by 1910. By the end of the twentieth century, cooking space again expanded and absorbed social functions, merging with family rooms and dining rooms. This trajectory follows changes in family structure, in the labor of cooking, in new inventions, and in the economies of diverse classes.

Early Cooking Spaces in Inventories and Archaeology

In a house where the two principal rooms were organized by rank—the ordinary furniture and activities in the hall separated from the special people, furnishings, and activities in the parlor—the milk-house or dairy presented an alternative organizational pattern: designating spaces by function. A milk-house is the name of one of the rooms in Thomas Beechar's Charlestown, Massachusetts house in a 1637 inventory where he stored butter, cheeses, and cheese-making equipment.[2] In this type of room dairy products would be kept cool, sometimes by digging the dairy into the ground by half a story or locating it in the cool cellar. Shelves built around the milk-house held butter or cheese, and trays of milk would cool there as cream rose to the top to be skimmed off for the churn. A window opening would allow light into the room as well as ventilation.

In the Chesapeake region and the southern colonies, the architecture of cooking was influenced by the region's commitment to an agricultural economy based on enslaved and indentured labor. Well-to-do planters provided a home for their immediate families in the main house. The kitchen with its indentured or enslaved laborers and hazardous sparks occupied a building of its own. Many additional storage and utility buildings dotted the near landscape. Enslaved workers and servants utilized the upper floors of separate outbuildings for sleeping. Travelers described the planter's house and home grounds as looking like a little village.

At the Clifts Plantation in Virginia, home to well-to-do tenants in the late seventeenth century, archaeology at the "manner house" has revealed

Fig. 1. The freestanding brick kitchen behind the Brush-Everard House in Colonial Williamsburg, Virginia, is one of several typical outbuildings constructed near Chesapeake houses. Outbuildings supported diverse food-related functions: a smokehouse to preserve meats, a dairy for milk products, a spring house, an ice house, a cool root cellar. Photo E. C. Cromley.

several types of food-related construction.[3] A hall and a chamber, both rooms heated by fireplaces, comprised the principal rooms of the original one-story house. The separate 1685 servants' quarter also contained two rooms and a fireplace. Food could have been cooked in either hall fireplace. Two smoke houses used for preserving meats were located near the servants' quarter. A newer quarter built about 1700 contained a kitchen with a storage cellar beneath it, separate from the main house. Now cooking could take place in a dedicated kitchen apart from the main house. A small outbuilding behind that house was used as a dairy to preserve milk products. For winter food storage, a root cellar beneath the house was constructed in 1725 and lined with brick. With all of these external food-related facilities in place, the hall of the main house could be used mainly for dining instead of cooking, so this room became increasingly formal and public.[4] Thus the main house stood at the center of a constellation of food-axis elements: smoke house, root cellar, kitchen, and servants' quarters all supported the production of meals.

Robert Beverley, author of the 1705 *History and Present State of Virginia*, observed that Virginia house builders separated food-related work from their dwelling spaces. "All their Drudgeries of Cooking, Washing, Daries [*sic*], &c. are perform'd in Offices detacht from the Dwelling-Houses, which by this means are kept more cool and Sweet."[5]

One example of this detachment of function-specific rooms from the dwelling can be seen at the restored Brush-Everard House in Williamsburg, Virginia of 1717. One of several outbuildings behind it is a kitchen constructed in 1750, a freestanding building of brick with a very large chimney to serve its cooking fireplace and bake oven. While the owner's house was built of wood, the kitchen is all masonry to assure that it would be fireproof. There are utilitarian reasons why kitchens were placed behind the main house, as Beverley observed. Perhaps even more important, however, was separating the conceptually clean reception rooms of the house from the conceptually dirty and messy food preparation areas, particularly when they were the zone of servants' and enslaved peoples' work.

Eighteenth-Century Cooking Spaces

Cooking inside eighteenth-century houses continued to be done over the fire in a wide fireplace. Many New Englanders constructed lean-to additions to houses in the early eighteenth century, which expanded the cooking and food-related spaces inside the house. When unheated, the lean-

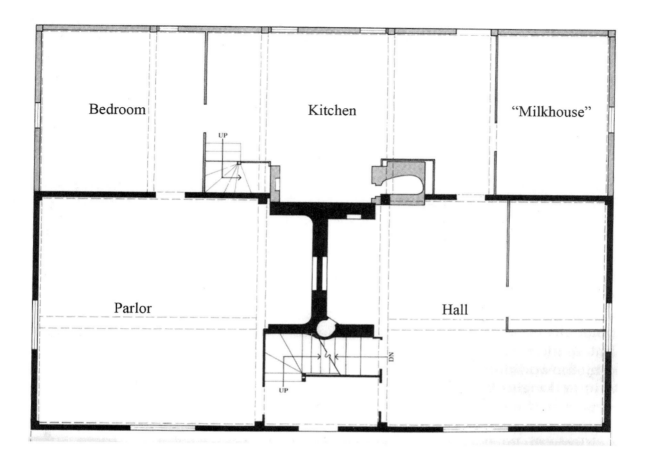

Fig. 2. Plan of the Boardman House with its 1690s lean-to addition on the back. Many householders included a new kitchen fireplace in the lean-to, freeing up the original hall to serve for light household production and sleeping. In the lean-to, one room was called a milkhouse and one a bedroom. Drawing from Abbott Lowell Cummings, *Framed Houses of Massachusetts Bay* (Cambridge: Harvard Univ. Press, 1979), 24.

to provided space for cool food storage. Sometimes, as at the Boardman House, they went to the expense of building a new kitchen fireplace there. Historian Abbott Cummings investigated numerous inventories of the seventeenth and eighteenth centuries to try to pin down where New Englanders did their cooking. Upon first consideration, it seemed that adding a lean-to probably meant separating out kitchen functions from the hall and giving them a dedicated space, but Cummings's study of inventories of fireplace equipment kept in the various rooms of early houses suggests that cooking hearths often remained in the hall well into the eighteenth century.[6]

Some Pennsylvania-German kitchens contained a more convenient raised hearth, which allowed the cook to stand while tending the meal, in contrast to cooking fireplaces in Anglo and Dutch settlement areas where builders usually located the fire on the floor level of the hall or kitchen, requiring the cook to stoop or kneel. Such hearths were built in Germany in the seventeenth century and brought to Pennsylvania by immigrants in

the seventeenth and eighteenth centuries. Travelers recorded seeing raised hearths in Pennsylvania-German houses, although no original ones survive in houses today.[7] While a raised hearth seems to have offered significantly more convenience to the cook, the fact that raised hearths were not widely used indicates that convenience was not as highly valued as tradition.

Kitchens in the first half of the eighteenth century retained many of the features of the later seventeenth century—the large fireplace, movable storage furniture supplemented by built-in shelves, and a dependence on an external water supply. Refinements can be seen in the pantry, dairy, and buttery subdivisions of kitchen space where convenience does seem to have influenced kitchen planning. At the Winslow House in Marshfield, Massachusetts, a pair of kitchen service rooms—dairy and buttery—are reached from the kitchen by stairs leading half a level above and half a level below the kitchen floor. The house was built c. 1725 and these features appear to be original to it. The location of this pair of service rooms seems to consider the cook: not too far to go up or down stairs to fetch necessary ingredients for the meal being prepared. The lower room takes advantage of the cool, below-ground level for keeping dairy materials, while the upper room provides broad shelves for storing foodstuffs and equipment.

A similar convenient arrangement was constructed at the 1786 Burtch-Udall Homestead in Queechee, Vermont. A trio of doors led from the kitchen to an entryway with a door to the outdoors; to the cellar where food was stored in a vaulted room; and to a pantry on the kitchen level. The cook could retrieve cooled foodstuffs from the cellar, go out the back door

Fig. 3a and Fig. 3b. Dairy products needed to be kept clean and cool. The eighteenth-century Winslow House in Marshfield, Massachusetts located its buttery/dairy half a level down from the kitchen. This location took advantage of the cool temperatures underground while keeping the dairy goods near to the kitchen and the cook. Some preferred to keep their dairy goods in a freestanding outbuilding. This dairy building, c. 1800, is at Eyre Hall on the Eastern Shore of Maryland. Its extended roof shades the walls to keep them cool while vents at the top of the wall aid air circulation. Photos E. C. Cromley.

Fig. 4. Three doors in the kitchen of the 1786 Burtch-Udall Homestead in Queechee, Vermont, led to the cool cellar where food was stored, to the pantry, and to the outdoors where gardens grew food. Food was stored conveniently available to the kitchen, characteristic of northern houses, rather than being deployed in the near landscape in outbuildings. Photo E. C. Cromley.

to fetch something from the garden, or gather supplies from the pantry, all within a few steps of the cooking fire.

Later Eighteenth- and Nineteenth-Century Expansion of Cooking Spaces

The great houses of southern plantations in the later eighteenth century typically located the dining room in the central block of the house and the kitchen in one of the dependencies. In preparing a meal, servants would move through the landscape from the smoke house to the milk-house to the kitchen, traveling through outdoor and indoor space, up and down stairs. Servants delivering food from the kitchen had to traverse long corridors, move from one story of the house to another, or even cross outdoor space in order to bring meals to the table. The foods secured from storage buildings, prepared in kitchens, and delivered to dining rooms had quite a long way to travel.

Well-to-do families in late eighteenth-century Charleston, South Carolina developed a house type called the single house in which the main house was set perpendicular to the street edge at one corner of the lot, while behind it deep yards contained numerous service spaces. Appropriating the outbuilding idea that was common on rural plantations, they preserved many of the same functions and spatial segregations according to rank. These typically created a long tail of linked structures extending from the main house to the back of the lot arranged along the property line.

Among these structures were kitchen buildings with slave quarters above, supplemented by smoke houses and other food storage spaces.[8]

From 1750 to 1850, specifically designed food preparation and storage spaces which had earlier been refined for elite families now spread to middling households, who made frequent improvements to the food axis in both urban and rural settings and at all levels of the economy. Householders supported meals with gardens even in cities, growing their own vegetables and fruits. Storing foods was essential so that families could feed themselves beyond the growing season, using everything from a hole in the ground to cellars beneath the house or root cellars dug into the nearby landscape to store their foods.

The idea of a separate kitchen building with quarter above had been popular with wealthy households such as at Shirley Plantation in the mid-eighteenth century, and it was also popular with middling households. Some early nineteenth-century rural houses in the southern regions continued the separate-kitchen tradition. At President Andrew Jackson's Hermitage Plantation in Tennessee there were two principal log structures in use from 1804 to 1821. One of these, the West Cabin or Farm House, was lived in by the Jackson family. The East Cabin, twenty feet by forty feet with two end chimneys, served as the Jacksons' kitchen quarter, housing cooking as well as providing dwelling space for enslaved people.[9]

Similar to the way that the Jackson family detached cooking spaces

Fig. 5. A root cellar in Butte, Montana. Vegetables could be kept from spoiling if stored at a steady, cool temperature—the temperature of the earth four or five feet below the surface. Householders would dig their own root cellars into this cool zone, which allowed settlers in all parts of the country, and into the twentieth century, to keep foods cool in barrels, boxes, and other containers. Photo E. C. Cromley.

from their house, French settlers in the Mississippi valley built freestanding food preparation facilities to use in combination with those inside the main house. In Ste. Genevieve, Missouri, historic French houses such as the 1770 Bolduc House have been restored or reconstructed.[10] The food axis in the Bolduc House may have begun as a kitchen in the yard, a large porch or gallery workspace surrounding the house, and a food garden. The stone kitchen that occupies a corner of the gallery was added in 1820. In the nineteenth century the house was partitioned into two and acquired two interior kitchens serving the two households then residing there. Later during the house's 1950s reconstruction a separate bake-house was added—a copy of the French bake-house type built in nearby St. Louis—standing behind the service porch.

At the back of the house was a large garden in which produce was grown to feed the family.[11] The kitchen at the back of the main house operated in tandem with the rear porch, which served as a staging area for preparing items gathered from the garden before taking them into the kitchen. Likewise houses that originally had an outdoor bake-house would have used the porch as the link for carrying goods for baking to and from the indoor kitchen. The Bolduc back porch was furnished with a churn for making butter, suggesting a dairy activity happening on the porch instead of in a separate milk-house. The garden, the back porch, and the outdoor bake-house are all linked to each other. The kitchen inside the house is incomplete without these other components.

Householders with the fewest resources did not always build a kitchen, either inside the main house or in outbuildings, but instead cooked outdoors. At the Virginia plantation, Stratford, a cooking tripod and kettle were set up outside the kitchen. Enslaved servants who did not have access to the foods and equipment needed for individual servings used these outdoor kettles to make one-pot stews, soups, or porridges. Meals like this were sometimes eaten out of the pot, on bread instead of dinner plates, and outdoors.

Kitchens could migrate around a house as owners made changes and improvements to housework. The Hamilton Farm at Parker's Landing, Kentucky has a main house begun around 1811 with a hall-parlor division of space. The original cooking space would have been in the hall fireplace. A rear "ell," or wing—so called because it formed the plan into an L shape—was added to the original house around 1820, probably to house a kitchen. In the next decade, sometime before 1830, the owner added a "backhouse"

Fig. 6. A tripod held a kettle to cook one-pot meals, exhibited at the Virginia mansion, Stratford. Cooks with few resources may have used only this method; enslaved residents of large plantations cooked one-pot meals while their masters ate more delicately prepared foods cooked in indoor fireplaces. Photo E. C. Cromley.

to the end of the ell where a smoke house and a new kitchen shared the space. Now the kitchen had yet another home. Complementing the kitchen, a domed, limestone dry cellar was built sometime between 1830 and 1860 for food storage.[12] At this Kentucky farm the kitchen was moved three times in the course of twenty years within the family's expanding home. The kitchen moved to the back of the house each time, placing cooking farther away from parlors and polite spaces.

Fig. 7. At the Tobias Walker farm in Kennebunk, Maine, cooking was first located in the hall's fireplace in 1780. Additional resources led the family to add a new kitchen ell in 1825. They rebuilt the kitchen again in the 1840s to contain a new cast-iron cookstove. Each time, the kitchen was moved to the back, farther away from the polite parlor. Drawing by Thomas Hubka.

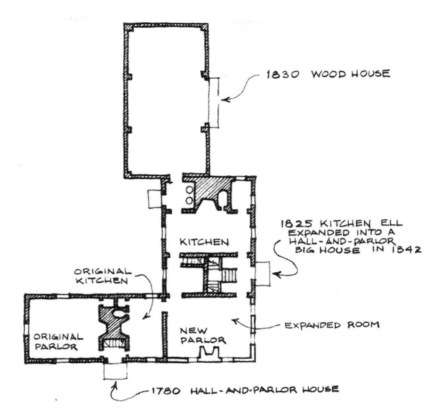

New England farmsteads show similar patterns of migrating kitchens. Thomas Hubka's research traced the kitchen's moves at the Tobias Walker farm in Kennebunk, Maine. In its original stage of development around 1780, cooking was located in the hall's fireplace. Additional resources led the family to add a new kitchen ell in 1825, which contained a larger cooking fireplace and large brick oven facing the front of the fireplace jamb. In the mid-nineteenth century it was becoming common to improve older kitchens with cast-iron cookstoves, which took up less room for cooking than the big fireplace. When the family again expanded their house in 1842 and added a cookstove, they reduced the size of the 1825 kitchen, yielding borrowed space for an indoor water closet and improved stairs to the upper floor.[13]

As house owners in the north gained more resources, they usually improved their houses by developing the food axis within the house instead of using outbuildings. Unlike some of their Chesapeake and South Carolina contemporaries, they typically did not choose the advantage of keeping heat and smells out in the backyard in an outdoor kitchen structure. Rather, they prioritized the advantage of locating meal preparation spaces very close to the rooms in which meals would be served, thereby assuring that foods would still be hot and fresh when they reached the table.

In his study of Franklin County, Massachusetts, Ritchie Garrison documents some typical kitchen ells. They contained the kitchen, pantry, buttery, woodshed, and often the privy, and some also included a dining room and a laundry.[14] Often in the later eighteenth century, kitchen ells were added onto existing houses or made integral to new builds. The ell was a rear addition and focused the cooking space of the house at the back, farther away from genteel entrance halls and parlors. Dr. Thomas Williams's house at Deerfield, Massachusetts for a well-to-do family had an ell addition built before 1775. More ells were constructed by central Massachusetts middling families in the 1820s to 1840s, such as at Samuel Stearns's house, completed in 1824, where there was an ell that housed the main kitchen, duplicating a full cellar kitchen.[15] An ell was also added to the rear of Elizabeth and Charles Phelps's farmhouse in 1771 in Hadley, Massachusetts. The original 1752, center-hall, ground floor of the dwelling was enlarged by more than 50 percent with the thirty-six-foot by twenty-foot ell. The new ell kitchen replaced one in the corner of the earlier house. In it was a new cooking fireplace with a much larger hearth, a pantry, and a "keeping" or multi-purpose room. In the attic above was a smoke chamber for preserving meat. The old kitchen then became a sitting room, a buffer between the fine front parlor and the ell in which servants worked.[16]

Introducing New Technologies

Changes in the arrangements of the food axis in the early nineteenth century arose from consolidating functions and from the introduction of new technologies. Gathering the spaces of spring house, smoke house, dairy, or root cellar into the main house or its ell enabled greater convenience, which was often tied to new technologies such as running water.

In 1807–8 a progressive owner, Merchant James Rundlett, added the latest kitchen technology to his house, the Rundlett-May House in Portsmouth, New Hampshire. He outfitted kitchen and rear ell with new kinds of cooking apparatus: in the kitchen an expensive Rumford roaster was installed to the left of the cooking fireplace, while to the right of the fireplace there was a bread oven accessible from the front. Adjoining this fireplace and oven to the right were three set kettles, each with its own firebox and vent. A hood above the kettles vented steam or smoke up through a flue. In the ell, another fireplace held hooks for suspending kettles over the fire and

Fig. 8. Merchant James Rundlett outfitted his kitchen and rear ell with new kinds of cooking apparatus at the 1807 Rundlett-May House in Portsmouth, New Hampshire. A special oven for roasting, another for bread, paired with the fireplace. Set kettles built in over fire compartments made it convenient to boil and simmer. Courtesty of Historic New England.

adjusting cooking heights. To the left was a set kettle with its own firebox and vent in which water could be boiled for cooking, laundry, and bathing purposes. Wooden shelves and cabinets lined the walls of both the ell and the kitchen proper for storing equipment. In back of the Rundlett-May House is a rear yard surrounded on three sides by a wood-shed, privies, a pig sty, and the carriage house. These linked structures create the enclosure for a courtyard that would have been used for messy housework and served as a drainage area for the set kettle in the ell.

Cellar kitchens became common in Portsmouth, New Hampshire after 1800, as historian Richard Candee documents, when the Portsmouth aqueduct was established to bring water directly into new houses. The Bernard-Lord House and the Laighton House are two examples of houses built before 1813 with cellar kitchens.[17] Their sloping sites were well-positioned to allow gravity to bring water from the aqueduct into their kitchens. The original owner of the first house, Samuel Barnard, advertised his house for sale in 1813 and described it as having an "excellent lower kitchen" which occupied half the cellar, with a roughly finished storage area in the other half. The Laighton House's cellar kitchen was accessed by means of a narrow stair in the central hall of the house. The room above the kitchen was finished with storage cabinets beside the fireplace, consistent with a dining room. By the mid-nineteenth century the family, tiring of

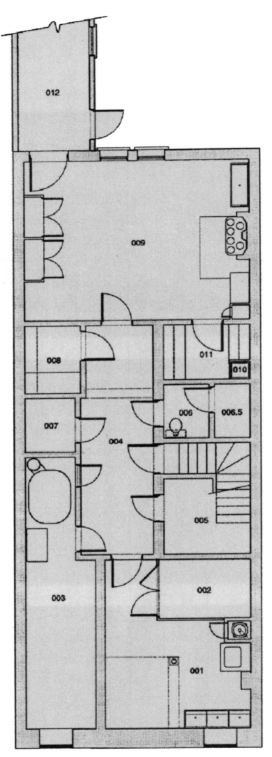

000 BASEMENT

001	LAUNDRY ROOM
002	DRYING ROOM
003	FURNACE ROOM
004	PASSAGE
005	STORAGE CLOSET, POSSIBLE MANSERVANT'S QUARTERS
006	SERVANTS TOILET
006.5	STORAGE
007	TRUNK STORAGE
008	KITCHEN STORAGE
009	KITCHEN, SERVANT LIVING AREA
010	DUMBWAITER
011	PANTRY
012	COAL SHED

0   5   10   15

the narrow stairway's inconvenience, renovated the house to relocate their kitchen in a rear ell, which placed cooking and dining on the same floor. Federal-period cellar kitchens were common in East-Coast cities and were mentioned by Norfolk, Virginia house renters such as Luke Wheeler and William Wirt who rented brick houses there at the turn of the eighteenth century.[18] On tight urban sites, cellars provided the extra space needed for housekeeping, while rural householders more often acquired extra rooms in ells by spreading out laterally, having access to more land.

Cellar kitchens remained popular in urban houses throughout the later nineteenth century, including those for elite households. The Gibson House in Boston's Back Bay of 1859 by Edward Cabot or the Charnley House of 1892 by Louis Sullivan and Frank Lloyd Wright in Chicago were houses built for wealthy clients. Both utilized a basement kitchen linked by a dumbwaiter to the butler's pantry and dining room above.

Competing with or supplementing the open cooking fire was a variety of iron cookstoves that came on the market from the early to the mid-nineteenth century. The first iron stoves, which served for both heating and cooking, were too expensive for any but wealthy customers. New American production methods after 1835 allowed stove parts to be cast in small furnaces located near consumers and thus reduced the price of a stove dramatically because it did not have to be transported from distant manufacturing sites.[19]

Built to contain an 1848 Walker's Range #7, a kitchen ell survives at the Farnsworth Homestead in Rockland, Maine. The house, built in 1849 in an unadventurous Greek Revival style, had an advanced kitchen. The new cookstove was heated by a coal fire, contained warming and baking ovens, and had five burners on top. Not only did it cook food, but this stove also helped to heat the house. In the bottom of the stove, coils heated water to be pumped to two bedrooms, the bathroom, and the kitchen sink. Later an 1868 radiator was installed in the upstairs bathroom, which was also fed hot water from the kitchen stove.[20]

Cooks discussed the virtues of either cooking in a fireplace or on a cookstove through the first decades of the nineteenth century. Did one or the other device produce the tastiest food? Cookbooks through the mid-nineteenth century included instructions for using both cooking devices. Historian Lynn Belluscio quotes a farmer writing to *The Genesee Farmer* in 1842 who felt that cheap farmhouses could be achieved now that the iron stove was easy to get and use, making fireplaces obsolete for heating and

Fig. 9. Opposite, The 1860 Gibson House in Boston, architect Edward Clarke Cabot. Separating the basement kitchen from the main-floor dining room was often necessary in urban settings where real estate pressures required smaller footprints for well-to-do houses. Upper-middle-class houses had servants to prepare meals in basement kitchens and serve them in main-floor dining rooms with the aid of a dumbwaiter.

Fig. 10. The Magee Grand range of 1894 represented the expensive end of iron cookstoves, which gradually replaced fireplace cooking. A kitchen ell survives at the Farnsworth Homestead in Rockland, Maine, built to contain an 1848 Walker's Range #7 of this size. Not only could this range cook generous meals on its five burners, but it also heated water for two bedrooms and a bathroom. Advertisement in *Boston Cooking School Magazine* 1 (Winter 1896–97): after p. 170.

cooking.[21] From the late eighteenth century to the mid-nineteenth century we can trace a shift from fireplace cooking with spits and utensils familiar from colonial days, to the introduction of cast-iron cookstoves and other new technologies in the kitchen.

At the same time, some impoverished households had no opportunities for improved kitchens. In African American educator Booker T. Washington's 1901 autobiography *Up from Slavery* he describes his pre-Civil War boyhood cabin on a Virginia plantation. His mother was the plantation cook, but there was no cooking stove on the plantation—all cooking was done over an open fire with pots and skillets. Washington remembered that the heat from the fireplace was hard to take during the summer.

Rural families had pressing needs to preserve food beyond the growing season to feed the family in the winter; to preserve these essentials, kitchens got especially heavy use during the summer months. The Von Der Ahe house in Molalla, Oregon, a modest 1860s farm house, had a freestanding summer kitchen for this purpose. It had four doors, one on each side, and not only did these doors guarantee access to the summer kitchen, but they also made certain that fresh breezes could blow through it so the cook was less overheated while working at the stove. Having a summer kitchen cleared workers, heat, and traffic from the main house's kitchen during the busiest cooking season.

Fig. 11. Tenement apartments for the working class with very few rooms compressed cooking, eating, and socializing into a single "living room." The cookstove and the rocking chair both find a home here in Vaux and Radford's tenements for the Improved Dwelling Association. Drawing in Elizabeth Bisland, "Cooperative Housekeeping in Tenements," *Cosmopolitan* 8 (November 1889): 36.

Cooking Challenges in Multi-Family Dwellings

Since cooking often produced messes, heat, and smells, householders separated their kitchens from the polite parts of the house—pushed to the rear, on a separate floor, or outside the main house. But what could they do if the dwelling was all on one floor and within a large apartment house? Urban apartment-house design in major American cities matured through the 1870s and 1880s. Expensive, large-scale apartment houses aimed to provide homes for upper-middle-class residents. To maintain the good manners that prescribed separating smelly cooking from elegant dining, the dining rooms in apartments were grouped with the other reception rooms like parlors and libraries, strictly separated from cooking. However, for more convenient food service, designers tried to bring kitchens and dining rooms into closer proximity to each other. Above all, apartment kitchens needed good ventilation, so they opened onto courtyards, air shafts, or backyards.

Both the specific conveniences for kitchen work and the names of rooms in which food-related activities took place distinguished the middle-class apartment dwelling from that of the working class in the later nineteenth century. New York City tenement apartments contained food preparation areas not in a separate kitchen, but in a room called the "living room," which contained a cast-iron cookstove. This room served as a social center for the household as well as a cooking and eating space. Journalist Jacob Riis's famous photographs of tenement dwellers in their homes show that piece work done for the garment trades would be executed in a living room, which also contained a large bed and a kitchen range.[22] Tenement dwellers would cook, dine, and perhaps also earn an income from boarders' rents or piece-work labor all in this one room instead of having the well-appointed kitchen available to higher income households.

Multiuse kitchens prevailed in Brownsville, New York tenements, as described in literary-critic Alfred Kazin's autobiography. He reported that the kitchen was always the center of the early twentieth-century tenement household. In his memoir, *A Walker in the City*, Kazin wrote: "As a child I felt that we lived in a kitchen to which four other rooms were annexed." The kitchen was where they ate all their meals. With a white tablecloth and company dishes for the Sabbath, Friday evening dinner was always served in the kitchen. After dinner the family went into the dining room and played games "at the dining-room table where we never dined," or listened to music on the victrola.[23]

Kazin's mother was a dressmaker. The sewing machine stood in the kitchen next to the cooking stove—their main source of heat. The kitchen where she worked all day was also where he did his homework. "By December the two outer bedrooms were closed off" when they became too cold to sleep in. Without a proper refrigerator, the family appropriated the bedrooms in winter to chill bottles of milk and cream, cold borscht, and jellied calves' feet. Kazin remembered, "In winter I often had a bed made up for me on three kitchen chairs near the stove."[24]

Modern Conveniences, Modern Cooking Process

In the early twentieth century, the kitchen was the entry point of a modern attitude inspired by the most efficient industrial processes. Modern efficiency was publicized by home economists who studied the ways that kitchen work could be accomplished most effectively in a small space. Utilities introduced in the nineteenth century such as plumbing for water and gas and later wiring for electricity became more widespread in this era, changing assumptions about the infrastructure desirable to support the food axis in a household. Preserving foods, which once had required specialized rooms or outbuildings, could now be done with electric appliances, while commercially preserved foods in cans or packages purchased from a grocer reduced the extent to which households had to preserve their own.

Home economics, the scientific study of home management, became popular in the early twentieth century as an attempt to professionalize women's work in the house and make it as efficient and as valued as men's work in factories and offices. Catharine Beecher had published her *Treatise on Domestic Economy* in 1841, explaining the duties of a good housewife and providing instruction so female householders could be more skilled at their jobs. She and her sister Harriet Beecher Stowe focused their attention on how houses performed for their users in their 1869 book *American Woman's Home*.[25] Making the kitchen as small as possible and providing a storage place for every piece of equipment and every foodstuff made their kitchen perform like a machine. Because housewives spent so much time in the kitchen, they located the nursery room nearby so the housewife could also be an efficient mother.

Beecher's prescient proposal anticipated the home economists' recommendations for efficient kitchens of the 1910s and 1920s. Home economists spoke of the kitchen as being organized to perform like a machine, honoring science and the ideals of Frederick Winslow Taylor and his ideas for streamlining factory work. Time and motion studies of factory work were borrowed by industrial engineer Lillian Gilbreth to map every movement used in meal preparation. Identifying the major appliances and how they were used in the preparation of a meal, they came up with the idea of a "work triangle" reflecting the most efficient path of movement from the range to the sink to the ice-box or refrigerator. Instead of a sentimentalized nurturing mother, the Victorian ideal, they envisioned a professional housekeeper and mother whose machines put her on par with industrial paid workers.

Anticipating the home economists' advice, urban and suburban single-family houses in the 1890s exhibit a new interest in kitchen convenience. At the Van Dyck house in New Brunswick, New Jersey, architect Frank Lent designed a very efficient food service area. At the rear of the house a generously sized kitchen opened onto a service porch with access to the cellar; the kitchen itself had a built-in sink and stove. As a link between the kitchen and the dining room a butler's pantry provided additional china and silver storage and washing-up space in another sink. The butler's pantry also provided a kind of air lock or valve between the smells of the kitchen and clean

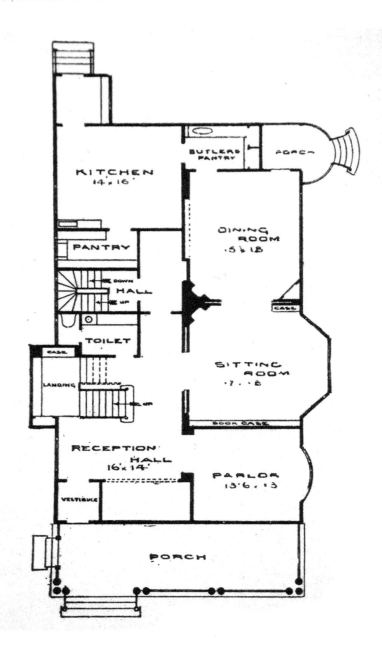

Fig. 12. Suburban houses for the upper middle class provided butler's pantries both for the storage of china, silver, glassware, and other table equipment as well as to provide a buffer between the noises and smell of the kitchen and the clean perfection of the dining room. Frank Lent's c. 1890 design for the butler's pantry at the Van Dyck house in New Jersey is an example. Lent, *Sound Sense in Suburban Architecture* (Cranford, NJ: self-published, 1893), 34–35.

perfection of the dining room. In the basement below the kitchen was a laundry room and a toilet.[26]

For average families, greater economy in the arrangement of space marks the change from 1900 to 1920. An "Inexpensive Suburban Home" of 1912 represents the new model. The small efficient house designed for the lower-income market was compact and presented a porch to the street. The first room encountered inside the front door and entry hall was a liv-

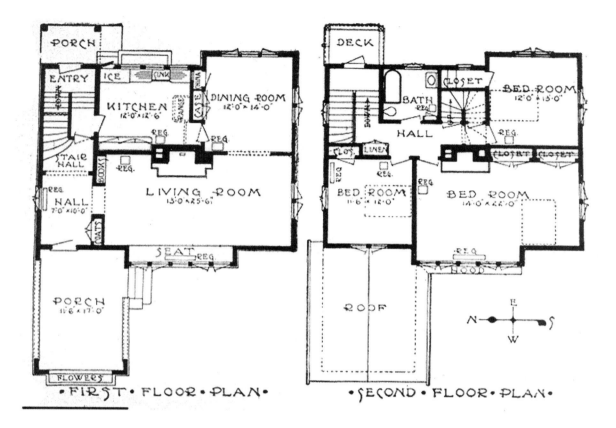

·FIRST·FLOOR·PLAN·   ·SECOND·FLOOR·PLAN·

Fig. 13. Home economists' recommendations for efficient kitchens resulted in small, compact rooms with well-thought-out shelves and cupboards. One side of Isabel Bevier's kitchen in her "inexpensive suburban home" has a counter with built-in upper and lower cabinets, while the dining room has two built-in case pieces for china, silver, linens, and glassware. Isabel Bevier, *Handbook of Housekeeping* (Chicago: American School of Home Economics, 1912), 84.

ing room—the newly informal replacement for the parlor. At the rear of the house was a small, efficient kitchen measuring twelve by twelve and a half feet and an adjacent dining room at twelve by fourteen feet. Appliances in the kitchen—an ice-box, a range, a sink—would have replaced any external food storage. The cottage's basement could incorporate food-storage space with shelves to hold preserved and canned foods, stretching the food axis to the basement level.

This early twentieth-century period is the apex of consolidation. All the separate cooking and food-preservation elements from the past—fireplace, root cellar, smoke house, spring house, dairy—are now found inside the kitchen. They take the form of refrigerators, running water in plumbed sinks, gas or electric ranges with cook-tops and ovens all in one. Formerly large food-preservation facilities have been miniaturized and domesticated. Magazines such as the *Ladies Home Journal* popularized this consolidation by reproducing house designs for their readership. Housewives reading such magazines would see how the economical attitude could be realized

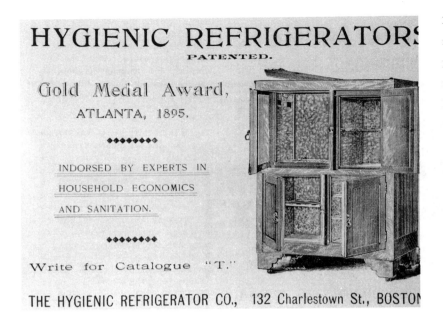

Fig. 14. Ice-boxes, also called refrigerators, brought cool food preservation into the kitchen and replaced dispersed dairies, ice-houses, and root cellars. Many new houses of the 1910s and 1920s supplied a little door on the back porch through which the iceman could deliver a weekly block of ice to this container. Advertisement in *Boston Cooking School Magazine* 1 (Winter 1896–97): after p. 170.

in new physical space arrangements, resulting in very small but satisfying houses.

Messy food preparation might be kept outside on a rear porch. In Melinda Haynes's novel *Mother of Pearl*, protagonist Luvenia Korner's father William built a new house in 1912. A simple ten-by-ten-foot porch at the back was called the "peeling platform," where Luvenia peeled potatoes, shucked beans, and plucked chickens. She also slept on the porch under a tent when the house was overcrowded on holidays. When the family enclosed the porch and put up a roof and screens, they renamed it "the dry porch," but it was still the site of peeling, shucking and plucking—keeping the really dirty work out of the kitchen.[27]

Housekeeping authority Lydia Ray Balderston's idea of a well-arranged small kitchen in 1919 included many features that still seem modern. Along one entire wall, built-in cabinets and drawers introduced convenient storage. Along another wall was a very long sink with hot and cold running water, well lit by three windows above it. In the center of the floor was an island with a smooth work surface on the top. Opposite the wall of cabinets was a cooking stove. Many of its principles are still favored in the design of twenty-first-century kitchens: the central island is very commonly found, windows above the sink are standard, and built-in cabinets—sometimes floor to ceiling—are expected elements in the contemporary kitchen.[28]

Cooking Space in Rural Houses

During the nineteenth century, settlers pushed into land west of the Appalachians to establish themselves at new farms and towns, taking the minimum of baggage with them. Although residents of more settled towns and cities had cooked in more advanced kitchens, when they left for their new life they returned to earlier technologies and less refined spaces. European immigrants flooded into the American frontiers as well, bringing with them their own heritage of farm or town kitchens. Sometimes the first house built for a family—perhaps a log house—was preserved to become a service building when the family's resources improved. As families expanded their houses, food preparation functions migrated around the homesite.

Norwegian immigrants traveled to the interior of the United States in the 1840s, settled on the northern frontier in Wisconsin, and built themselves log houses. One such house, built for the Fossebrekke family, has been restored and resides at an outdoor museum, Old World Wisconsin. It has one room on the ground floor and a second unfinished room in the attic. The family used a cooking vessel suspended from a tripod outside the one front door.

Living in structures of only one room, built of log, lumber, or other materials at hand, rural residents lacked the differentiated spaces that Americans had experienced in the more established areas of settlement. Unlike seventeenth-century newcomers, however, these householders were acquainted with the new conveniences that industry produced and often were able to acquire one or two elements of modern food apparatus, in spite of their rustic circumstances. Canned goods and cookstoves made their way to rural cabins, even if function-specific separate rooms did not. Quickly built shelters supplied very few conveniences.

Vivid descriptions of their frontier dwelling are preserved in Edith Kohl's memoir of homesteading on the South Dakota frontier, where Edith and her sister settled in 1907.[29] When they arrived, they discovered that the house they had purchased—sight unseen—was a tarpapered shack that "looked like a large but none too substantial packing-box tossed haphazardly on the prairie." Claim shacks had typical dimensions of nine by twelve feet, twelve by twelve feet, or twelve by fourteen feet for the whole house—compare these to typical dimensions for efficient kitchens on the East Coast or in midwestern suburbs. A small oil stove, a box used for a cupboard, and two

Fig. 15. The Kohl sisters, homesteading on the South Dakota frontier, lived in this small shack of c. 1908 on the prairie. The shack has no separate kitchen. Refrigeration was only achieved by keeping foods outdoors. The sisters made use of canned foods while waiting for their first crops to grow. Edith Eudora Kohl, *Land of the Burnt Thigh* (New York: Funk and Wagnalls, 1938; repr., St. Paul: Minnesota Historical Society Press, 1986), 16.

homemade chairs comprised the rest of the furnishings. Necessary small cookstoves burned twists of hay or buffalo chips (coal and wood being very scarce). An old trunk placed outdoors had to serve as a refrigerator.[30]

The period desire for small kitchen spaces was satisfied by the little claim shack, but there were hardly enough resources to worry about the efficiency of the cook. When the Kohl sisters got a new claim of land in South Dakota in the early twentieth century, they added a six-by-eight-foot shed-roofed kitchen to the back of their shack and furnished it with a new cookstove that included an oven.[31] They recapitulated the pattern familiar from a hundred years earlier at the turn of the nineteenth century when house owners had had their first access to cookstoves and built kitchen ells on the backs of houses to contain them.

The Kohl sisters found that there was nowhere for South Dakota homesteaders to buy vegetables until the crops matured. Since fresh foods were very hard to come by, canned goods supplied the settlers' needs. "It is a curious paradox that people living on the land depended for food or canned goods from the cities, and that the fresh milk and cream and green vegetables associated with farm life were unattainable." That left settlers living on dried fruits, beans and potatoes, and canned goods. Many homesteaders did not make it and their abandoned shacks were visible all over the prairie surrounded by tin cans, for "as a rule the shack dwellers lived out of tin cans like city apartment dwellers."[32]

The characteristically restricted kitchen square footage of frontier houses required food spaces to accommodate both cooking and dining, plus additional uses such as sewing or relaxing for a moment in the rocking chair.[33] A woman who lived in a North Dakota frontier sod house from 1908 to 1916 described her dwelling as having two main spaces: one contained three or four beds, and the other "held a kitchen range, a table for nine people, a sewing machine," and a rocking chair. Underneath the kitchen was a small cellar used for storing produce.[34] Additional multiuse kitchens in houses of the upper Midwest can be found in Fred Peterson's *Homes in the Heartland*. The efficiency recommended by home economists that depended upon eliminating all extraneous uses from the kitchen was clearly not possible in these houses, since there were only two rooms to contain all functions. Late twentieth-century kitchen designers have reveled in incorporating multiple uses in the kitchen-greatroom, a mixture that was anathema to the theorists of good kitchen practice in the 1910s and 1920s.

Even when their houses had sufficient rooms to allow a clear differentiation of functions, some ethnic groups preferred to retain sociable, rather than efficient, kitchens when they settled in America. Slate miners and their families who had emigrated from Italy and settled in Roseto, Pennsylvania built modest, working-class houses starting in the late 1880s. Most older Roseto settlers' houses followed contemporary lower-cost house types with a living room and a kitchen on the ground floor, and two or three bedrooms and the bathroom on the second floor. The kitchens were large and used as family rooms; the living rooms were never used except for guests and special occasions. In addition to the generous kitchen space, these households also used the basement as an essential part of the food axis. In the basement there were rooms for wine making and food storage, with shelves on which they stored "hundreds of jars with home-canned vegetables and fruit."[35] Home canning implies another element of the food axis—a garden beside the house—as working-class residents made the most of their real estate to supply their food needs.

Twentieth-Century Cooking Space

Model kitchen room layouts were provided in a 1918 book, *Mechanics of the Household*. In this model, two sinks with running water for 1) laundry and 2) meal preparation and clean-up were installed next to a hot water tank. Adjacent to the hot water tank was a coal-fired range. Next to that was a radiator, indicating that the house had central heating. Although the under-decorated kitchen looked primitive, having little in it besides plumbing and heating appliances, a chair, and a table, it nonetheless ran on

Fig. 16. New electric appliances like this 1927 refrigerator made the 1920s kitchen more modern and dependent on external power. Electric cooking implements—coffee pots, frying pans, and chafing dishes—also brought certain kinds of cooking into the dining room. Photo E. C. Cromley.

Fig. 17. Early twentieth-century kitchens typically positioned each appliance—sink, stove, ice-box— apart from each other (from E. S. Keene, *Mechanics of the Household* [1918], 95). The shelves, cupboards, and counters that we typically see framing kitchen appliances now were housed in the pantry, not the kitchen.

modern utilities. Conceived of as part of several domestic systems—the central heating system, a hot and cold water delivery system, and a wastewater system—this model kitchen represents a modern attitude toward household infrastructure.

The appliances and furnishings of the 1920s kitchen were transformed from their nineteenth-century predecessors as electric power became available to the average town-dweller. "Now that the seeming miracle of washing, cooking, sweeping, sewing and dishwashing by electricity has been accomplished, the restless American mind is inquiring whether domestic refrigeration by electricity is practicable," wondered a 1920 journalist in *House Beautiful*.[36] Refrigerators with artificial cooling systems replaced the ice in the ice-box beginning in the late 1920s. "It looks as if the iceless refrigerator—along with the horseless carriage, wireless telephone and fireless cooker—has come to stay," wrote the same journalist. By 1923 electricity was included in the US standard of living index as an expected domestic utility, and small electric motors were now powering kitchen appliances, sewing machines, and vacuum cleaners.

Although apartments had provided affordable homes for urban families in the post-World War II era, ownership of a single-family house was clearly the preferred model. The builder William Levitt created three postwar developments called Levittowns in New York, New Jersey, and Pennsylvania in the late 1940s and 1950s. The Levittown on Long Island, begun in 1947, saw forty-two hundred new, freestanding, single-family houses produced in one year, originally as rentals. There a typical Levitt house was a

Fig. 18. In contrast to freestanding appliances of the past, modern aesthetics required continuous surfaces and planes for kitchen cabinets and counters. Appliances are woven into the counters and cabinets for an integrated whole. This kitchen is obviously easier to clean. *Sears Roebuck Catalog* (Fall 1951): 1028.

Cape Cod–style house with about 750 square feet of space inside. It contained a kitchen at ten by ten feet, with built-in cabinets, appliances, and a back door; a living room at twelve by sixteen feet, with a front entrance; no dining room; two bedrooms, and a bathroom.[37] The standard Levittown kitchen had white enameled appliances and metal cabinets with a black tile floor. Like the upper-middle-class houses illustrated in professional magazines like *Architectural Record*, Levitt's houses also had continuous countertops and upper and lower kitchen cabinets.

In 1951 a kitchen illustrated in the Sears Roebuck catalog frames the housewife with upper cabinets, the continuous countertop, lower cabinets, and a linoleum floor. Garbed in her apron, the housewife bridges the historic gap between the metaphorical cleanliness of the dining space and the metaphorical dirt of the food preparation area. The smooth continuity of line that wrapped all appliances and storage functions into one coherent formal solution coincides with another continuity in the arena of the housewife's identity: now that she does all the housework herself, her duties erased the distinction between servant and hostess.

There has been a recent trend among wealthier house owners to build second and even third indoor kitchens. The idea of having a second kitchen in a house has often been appealing; in the eighteenth century as we have seen, some householders had an outdoor kitchen and an indoor one. Others had a summer kitchen in the basement and a winter kitchen on the main floor.

Variations of this double kitchen were used in the nineteenth century up and down the Eastern Seaboard and in other areas of the country. In the new suburbs around Washington, DC some recent multimillion-dollar houses are also provided with two kitchens, but for somewhat different reasons. An article in the *Washington Post* explained that developers building houses costing more than $3 million include a beautifully appointed kitchen at the rear of the house paired with a second kitchen accessible via a sliding door from the main kitchen. "Appliances have become so sleek, cabinetry so elegant; counter topping . . . so much like sculpture; and design so sophisticated that contemporary kitchens look too good to use."[38] Victorian parlors, as we will see, shared this property of being too good to use.

The family that has the too-beautiful principal kitchen has a second kitchen that caterers use during parties. The main kitchen's wood features are elegant cherry while the second kitchen is done in pedestrian pine. Guests congregate in the main kitchen and admire the design and fine materials, while the help prepare their food in the pine kitchen.[39]

Such "show" kitchens are not just the province of the wealthy; because particularly messy or intense cooking is characteristic of various ethnic groups, many have preserved the habit of a second kitchen. In Chinese families, the wok kitchen may be located in the basement or in an outbuilding to keep the smells and dirt associated with preparing food in hot oil out of the family's everyday kitchen. Italian families who prepare an annual stock of tomato sauce keep a basement kitchen for the intense cooking necessary when a tomato harvest must be preserved. Greek families who make their own wine do so in the basement's second kitchen.

Dorothy Baumhoff built a new house for her family near Boise, Idaho in the 1980s. Appearing on television's food channel, she explained how she designed a second kitchen in the basement especially for canning fruits and making jams and jellies.[40] Realtor Linda Morelli reports that lower-middle-class householders in Massachusetts and Connecticut quite often constructed a second kitchen in the basement, arrangements she observes when families put their houses on the market for her to sell. The real dirty work of everyday food preparation could be done in the basement kitchen, preserving the main floor kitchen as a hospitable space ready for visitors.

Recent immigrants to the United States occupying houses originally built for American cooking have adapted them to their particular ethnic cooking and lifestyles.[41] The Chinese immigrant casino workers who have settled in Connecticut have adapted standard American single-family, ranch, and split-level houses. They use the former lawn in the front of the house as a location for growing specialized vegetables such as winter melons and dry fish on outdoor lines where clothes might have normally dried. Since these houses are often occupied by several unrelated people rather than a single family, occupants have built walls to increase separation, cutting off a section of a formerly roomy kitchen, for example, to produce a smaller kitchen and an adjacent eating room or even an extra bedroom.[42]

Because cooking requires fire and the safety precautions that come with it, cooking spaces inside houses have been purpose-built. While some people managed to cook outdoors in a pot hung from a tripod or over a campfire, safety required people within houses to build a fireplace and a chimney whenever possible, or later to confine their fires to a cookstove or yet later a kitchen range. Unlike sleepers who can snooze in any room of a house, those preparing food have always had to observe constraints. The need for safe food storage inspired numerous solutions such as taking advantage of cool, underground temperatures; using the preservative features of smoking and salting; and the development of the electric refrigerator. Ethnic preferences in food production have led to adaptations from the American norm such as second, basement kitchens for messy cooking. Only in the late twentieth and twenty-first centuries, when modern tools such as the microwave oven have eliminated fire as the heat source, have householders enjoyed more latitude in the indoor location for cooking.

2

SOCIALIZING: PARLOR, LIVING ROOM, FAMILY ROOM, LIVING-KITCHEN

Inviting friends and family members to visit one's house suggests the need for a dedicated place to offer sociability. The most familiar such room in modern times is the living room, often paired with a family room, where people hang out, informally socialize, or more formally entertain. Comfortable couches, easy chairs, and small tables combined with lamps for pleasant lighting make a living room relaxed and inviting. Often a living room is adjacent to or combined with a family room, providing space for recreational television and snacks.

"Parlor" is the favored term for the seventeenth-century reception room as well as the Victorian social space, while "living room" came into use as a late nineteenth-century name for such an area. "Family room" describes informal social space—a usage beginning in later nineteenth-century middle-class houses; "great room" renames such spaces in larger, late twentieth-century houses, nostalgically reviving a colonial-era name for a general-purpose room. But historically, spaces for receiving friends and family range broadly, from one corner of a single-room cabin, to a formal parlor in an urban row house, to a themed rec room in a 1950s finished basement, to a stool pulled up to a counter in a busy living-kitchen. Social class, income, and local custom frame which kinds of spaces are suitable for socializing and entertaining in any particular time period, and what they should be called.[1]

One-Room to Multi-Room Sociability

Five centuries ago, the first European settlers building houses in the New World put expediency first and had no social room separate from the rest of their daily living space. The seventeenth-century governor of the territory that is now Texas lived in a house comprising a single room.[2] Meals were served to visitors in that room or outdoors, and those invited to spend the

Fig. 19. The 1840s Veggli House at Old World Wisconsin. A one-room cabin compresses all social life and work into a single undifferentiated space with a single door. Photo E. C. Cromley.

night slept on built-in bunks around its walls. Privacy and the separation of one activity from another was not considered. Combining all functions into a single room was common in eras when money to build was scant: seventeenth- and eighteenth-century settlers built one-room houses in Massachusetts, as did Ohio frontier cabin-builders in the later nineteenth century.[3] Limitations on space forced residents to collapse their multiple activities into a small compass; urban studio apartments or contemporary "tiny houses" work the same way in the early twenty-first century.[4]

When New Englanders or residents of the Chesapeake region could afford to expand their early-house ground floors from one to two rooms, they often chose to differentiate the two rooms by assigning ordinary, daily-life activity to one room—the hall—and special, higher-ranking life to the other—the parlor or chamber. Yet both these rooms included sociable visiting and entertaining like a modern living room. Rooms used for sociability in these early years contained what we would now call mixed uses. Like one-room houses, two-room houses included eating, socializing, and sleeping activity in both rooms. The two-room division allowed a shift from ordinary residents and their housework and interactions in the hall to higher-ranking persons, higher-quality furniture, tableware, and textiles, and more ceremonial parties and dinners in the parlor. There was no one room set aside for the specific function of socializing in the manner of a Victorian parlor.

Fig. 20. Overview of Shirley Plantation in Virginia, a large plantation house with social spaces in the main block. The more the many work-specific spaces were separated from the main house in outbuildings, the more the main house could have spaces dedicated to sociability. Eighteenth-century great houses focused decoration and fine furnishings on parlors and dining rooms, where social life flourished. Drawing by R. Frangiamore, *Antiques* (February 1973).

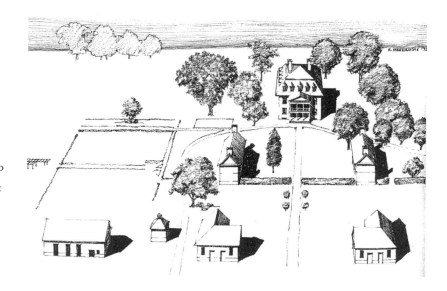

When New England householders became more prosperous and decided to add a third room to the ground floor, it often had the purpose of removing the cooking from the hall's sociable space (see fig. 2 in chapter 1). Separating food-related dirt, smells, and heat from social interactions paved the way toward eventually creating rooms purely for socializing.

When we try to imagine how people of the past used their social rooms, we can get clues from the furniture and other goods they kept there. Beth Twiss-Garrity studied eighteenth-century house inventories from rural Delaware. She showed that people were making an effort to rationalize the uses of individual rooms and create specialized social rooms even when they had too few rooms to really do the job. Mary Alston's Delaware house had a hall and a parlor, a kitchen and a loft. She tried to arrange her furniture so as to create a proper dining room in her hall, but as a result had to put all five of her beds in the parlor. This created a specialized sleeping room, but the parlor then failed as a sociable room.[5]

Great households of the plantation-owning class, from the Chesapeake region to Louisiana, made entertaining visitors a serious undertaking. Because these houses tended to be located at a distance from each other across rural landscapes, rather than close to each other such as on Boston or New York streets, family and friends who came to visit stayed for extended periods of time. Those who could afford to expanded their houses to accommodate such guests. George Washington's Mt. Vernon in Virginia is a well-known example of a large house with several dedicated rooms for social occasions; removing work spaces from the main body of the house preserved the gentility of its social spaces. A suite of outbuildings to contain utilitarian housework frames the main house. Segregating the heat and mess of cooking in an external kitchen helped keep the main house cool, and segregating servants—enslaved or free—in external service spaces away from the social space of the house protected family and guests from mixing with people they felt to be their inferiors.

The Proper Parlor of the Nineteenth Century

Formal parlors took on the purified function of sociability for middle- and upper-middle-class nineteenth-century householders.[6] Separate outbuildings had housed work-related activity in agricultural settings, leaving the main house to serve sociability. But in suburban and urban settings, and increasingly in the main house on plantations, those functions were consolidated and assigned their own rooms inside houses. With many disparate functions now located within the main house, sociability needed to be proclaimed in its own space and protected.

In the parlor, visitors would be introduced to the character and quality of the household by means of its best furniture, pictures, and ornaments. Elite households maintained schedules for visiting days and formal receptions, keeping the front parlor always ready to impress guests. Proper manners guided the behavior of parlor seating arrangements and conversations. In urban settings, row houses—a tall, narrow, and deep house type—located parlors as street-facing front rooms. In suburban settings, houses used room plans more spread out on the landscape, but they equally foregrounded the proper parlor. Most other functions were purged from the parlor and given their own rooms: formal dining rooms served for feeding the family and entertaining guests; separate kitchens and pantries supported servants cooking meals; and bedrooms contained sleeping, wardrobe storage, and dressing.

Urban row houses often had a front and a back parlor. This divided room allowed stricter rules of decorum and decoration in the front when separated from the back parlor by sliding doors. The front parlor contained expensive decorations such as paintings, rich carpets, drapes at the windows, and upholstered furniture. Dark colors added richness to the effect, but also disguised the soot caused by coal fires and oil lamps. In the back parlor, children engaged in games and family activities while less fancy furnishings created a more relaxed atmosphere.

Fig. 21. Location of front and back parlor functions in an urban house shown on a drawing from Calvert Vaux. Front rooms, closest to the street, also called drawing rooms in the period, received guests and formal visits; libraries or back parlors, furnished more informally, accommodated family and children. *Villas and Cottages* (1864; reprint New York: Dover Publications), 323.

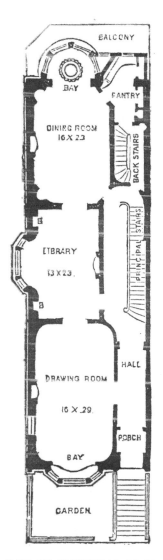

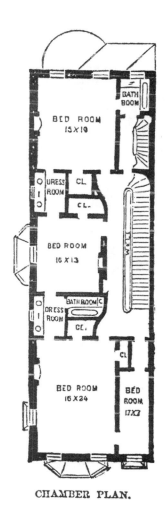

CHAMBER PLAN.

PLAN OF PRINCIPAL FLOOR.

A view of a mid-nineteenth-century parlor was published in *Gleason's Pictorial Drawing Room Companion* in 1854.[7] This parlor, in a merchant's mansion, is praised for its harmonious qualities of décor. "The room looks like a fitting abode of a man of refinement—a drawing room where a lady of elegant manners and educated taste might appropriately receive her guests." The magazine's writers deplore parlors with meaningless carving, excess gilding, and vulgar elaboration.

The parlor was the family's link to the outside world, the least "homey" of their otherwise private rooms. Victorian parlors were somewhat

Fig. 22. Gleason's "Parlor View in a New York Dwelling" shows decoration suitable for a Victorian-era, socially ambitious family. Parlors were reputed to be furnished so elaborately that the children of the family were afraid to enter. *Gleason's Drawing Room Companion* (Nov. 11, 1859): 300.

forbidding in their formal décor, but that made them suitable for "both weddings and funerals [that] occurred in the parlor." Displaying the embalmed deceased for viewings by family and friends gave a funerary use to the parlor in the Victorian era. A funeral held in the parlor "signified the last formal reception of guests by the deceased individual."[8] Likewise, weddings were held in parlors since they were occasions for the family to present its members to the community. The formality of the parlor suited the formality of wedding vows before witnesses.

This later nineteenth-century era sees the triumph of the formal parlor for middle- and upper-class householders. The parlor is a tool to present the owners' status to others, reminding themselves that they have achieved an important place in society. But it was a brief victory of formal manners and behavior. As life became increasingly informal in the 1880s and 1890s, the terms "family room" and "sitting room" began to supplement or replace the term "parlor" for the main socializing room.

The many architecture pattern books published in the nineteenth century allowed builders in all parts of the US to have house plans at hand that they would adapt to local materials and clients' demands.[9] Suburban house plans of the era show the presence of parlors, but also preserve a variety of other names for the social rooms in the house. We can trace the way that the name and character of a nineteenth-century parlor was thrown into question by reviewing the names on plans by architects of that era.

Fig. 23. Finding the idea of a parlor too stiff and old-fashioned, designers and their clients made an effort to find new conceptions and names for the social rooms in late nineteenth-century houses. The Boyce House, Chicago, by architect Francis Whitehouse, has neither a parlor nor a living room but instead a reception hall and a library. *Inland Architect* 21 (1893).

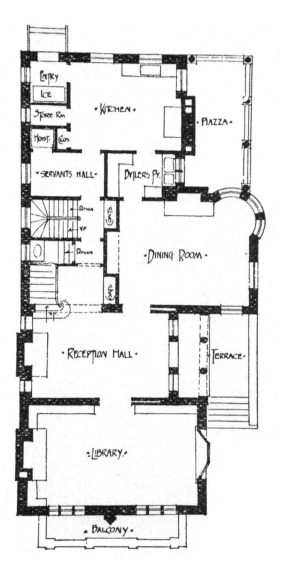

Openness to clients' needs encouraged the architect to suggest a variety of identities for the social rooms.[10] An example of a small house from 1875 included a room called "study" but which the designer E. C. Hussey said could equally serve as a library, office, sitting room, sewing room, or reception room. Charles Lakey's 1875 pattern book *Village and Country Houses* showed a "Cottage at Barrytown" that included both a "family room" and a "parlour" of identical dimensions. The family room was distinguished by a generous bay window affording views of the landscape.[11] Chicago architects Irving and Allen Pond's house at 620 Division Street at the corner of

Lake Shore Drive had a parlor, a dining room, and a study as the set of three ground-floor social rooms, while the C. H. Chandler house in Evanston—a suburb of Chicago—by Raeder, Coffin, and Crocker had a parlor, sitting room, and dining room. Also in Evanston, architects Raeder, Coffin, and Crocker designed a house in 1891. On the plan, they called their main living space a "sitting room," while the room called "parlor" was attached to the front hall and reception space associated with the more formal welcoming and sorting of visitors.[12] Edbrooke and Burnham's house for H. G. Chase had a library, drawing room, music room, and dining room but no parlor; while Treat and Folz's house for George B. Carpenter had a parlor, library, dining room, and music room—no study or sitting room. In the Chicago house of S. Leonard Boyce, architect Francis Whitehouse supplied a reception hall, a library, and a dining room, but there was no parlor, no drawing room, nor anything called "living room."

Chicago newspaper reporters in the society columns of the late 1880s and 1890s described Mrs. John Glessner's frequent teas and receptions in her house at 1800 Prairie Avenue, Chicago, as taking place in her "drawing room," but in her diary Mrs. Glessner referred to the same room as the parlor. When a close friend dropped in on her visiting day, he was received in the parlor, but he declared, "You won't make us stay in here, I want to go in the library," the more informal room, to better enjoy his visit.[13] The term "drawing room" indicated something more pretentious than Mrs. Glessner had in mind for her parlor, yet the parlor was a little too formal for her guest, who wanted the ease of the library for his visit.

According to architect Edward Young in an 1896 article, people needed to think carefully about their selection of social rooms when commissioning a house. Some people who were not well read might mistakenly leave "the library" out of a house, thinking that a sitting room, living room, or back parlor was a reasonable substitute. He declared that such a choice would only make the family look uneducated.[14] Young implied that house owners of the period experienced their social rooms under a floating array of names, selecting an identity for these spaces according to family taste and class; those who were not eager readers and did not aspire to raising their social status would think the library was the same as a sitting room.

The idea of comfort achieved by a relaxing of strict parlor manners led to adopting the name "living room." Even before the turn of the twentieth century, the formal parlor as the principal reception room was disappearing,

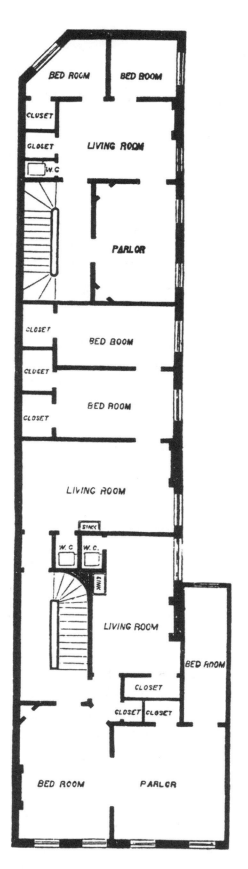

Fig. 24. Plan of a "cheap flat" for the working poor. In low-cost tenement buildings, a room called "living room" was the central all-purpose room in the apartment unit. There cooking, eating, and socializing activities combined with income-producing work and even sleeping. This plan for three flats per floor shows living rooms equipped with sinks and flues for cookstoves. Under the crowded conditions of working-class neighborhoods, the aspirational "parlor" would also serve as a bedroom. Richardson, "New Homes of New York," *Century* (1874): 64.

to be replaced by the title "living room" for the middle class as well as the working class. This is an example of an architectural idea moving up in social status rather than "trickling down." The Victorian parlor had had the principal job of presenting the family to the public—a public made up of visitors paying formal calls. A Victorian parlor had kept everyone, parents and children, on their stiff best behavior, while the modern living room allowed relaxation and promoted family togetherness.[15]

The term "living room" first became popular in nineteenth-century working-class tenements. In most early eighteenth-century American houses, a single room—the hall—had served as the all-purpose space where cooking, food storage, spinning or candle-making, sleeping, dining, and entertaining visitors all took place. Such a common room continued as the central space in working-class dwellings and tenement apartments, now under the name "living room." The single-floor designs for "Cheap Houses for Mechanics," published by Charles Lakey in his pattern book of 1875, had three- and four-room plans. The main room was marked "living room," with a separate kitchen and one or two bedrooms.[16] Not surprisingly, the room numbers and sizes in working-class dwellings were fewer and smaller than those for the middle-class.

While tenement breadwinners often worked in factories or made money from other jobs outside the home, the working-class living room was also a site for income-producing work. Men brought home the materials for cigar-making and rolled cigars in their living rooms. Women picked up pre-cut clothing parts from factories and sewed them together at home. Thus workers' housing served as live-work space in the late nineteenth and early twentieth centuries, a trend later seen at the turn of the twenty-first in some middle-class dwellings where workers used their homes as live-work spaces when they engaged in telecommuting labor.

While the New York reform tenements of the 1880s focused on a room called "living room," the central all-purpose room in the apartment unit, some late nineteenth-century tenement apartments also had a room labeled "parlor."[17] This may reflect the architect's encouraging tenants to aspire to middle-class standards, but tenement units with high occupancy rates could never afford to dedicate a room to socializing when the demand for sleeping and work spaces was so high.

The Parlor Dismissed for Twentieth-Century Households

The early twentieth-century bungalow era refocused its emphasis much more on the family members' own comfort and amusement. Bungalow living rooms are characteristically modest in size and well lit by windows. Living rooms often have some built-in furniture such as bookcases, shelves, and seats or benches near a fireplace—the inglenook—which saved space and created a cozy rather than imposing atmosphere. Lighter colors for walls and painted or natural woodwork complement much-simplified furniture styles. A leather and oak sofa by arts and crafts designer Gustave Stickley, for example, contrasts with a Victorian tufted velvet and carved rosewood parlor suite.

Overly decorated parlors became an object of concern in the household-advice columns of turn-of-the-century magazines because they were believed to drive the children out of the house. A house that was just a showcase for possessions is "quite unadapted to the family need of having a good time."[18] A parlor "for company only," or a bedroom kept "irksomely neat," provided nothing for a boy to do and nowhere to do his favorite things comfortably.

Fig. 25. Contrasting aesthetics—the carved rosewood chair with ornament typical of formal parlor furniture, proper posture, and good manners; the later Craftsman-style unornamented oak, where simple lines convey relaxation suitable for living or sitting rooms. Photo E. C. Cromley.

Writing on the subject in 1896, Mary Gay Humphreys advised that the home must cater both to "the interest of the family at large" and work "for the benefit of its members as individuals." To do this, it "ministers to physical comfort, contributes to mental satisfaction, and is the medium of individual expression." Humphreys theorized that the hall and drawing room or parlor are the rooms that especially pertain to relations between the family and society; the dining room and the "common room" or sitting room pertain to the family's closer relations; while the sleeping room pertains to the individual.[19]

Focusing on the purposes of the living room in 1922, the *Ladies Home Journal* magazine published advice on how to decorate a little house. Author Ethel Carpenter's article "The Living Room as the Heart of the Little House" found that it symbolized "enthralling hours of work and play, the companionship of family, the welcoming of friends, the tasks accomplished, the plans made, the books or music enjoyed in the firelight."[20] Unlike a nineteenth-century formal parlor, living rooms were for relaxed interac-

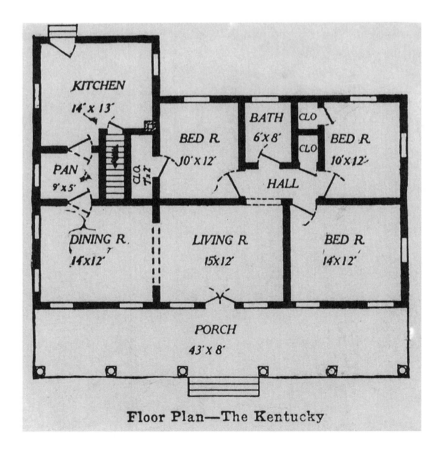

Fig. 26. Formal Victorian parlors were replaced by living rooms, which conveyed the informality characteristic of smaller and less expensive 1910s and 1920s houses. Bungalows such as the Kentucky by the Aladdin Co. appealed to a range of working- and middle-class residents in the early twentieth century. They preferred living rooms to parlors because such rooms seemed to represent family comfort. *Aladdin Homes* (Bay City, MI: 1919).

tions, not for display. She observed that the "living-room spirit" embodied "all sorts of plain things, such as comfort, convenience and use." In order to foster this comfort and convenience, she advised that there should be groupings of furniture, each focused around a lamp, so people could read, sew, knit, chat, play the piano, or work at the desk. A table at the side made a space for playing games. A living room, then, presupposed the gathering of family and friends together, including children. The activities included music and conversation but also small tasks like sewing or knitting, and quiet reading.

Post–World War II modernist architects developed the informal social possibilities sought by a middle- and upper-middle-class public.[21] In the forty houses illustrated in a 1948 *Architectural Forum*, every single house has a room called "living room." This room had unquestionably become the major social space for all classes of this era. It is also an open room with large windows whose space is enlarged by views of the landscape.[22] Some of the houses offer a room called "living/dining," where the dining area is just an offshoot of the living room, not contained by four walls but labeled as an "area" for dining.

The focused living room, designated for sociability, began to lose its focus and become diffuse as houses sported additional rooms for sociability. Additional rooms that also served a social purpose appear in postwar houses under diverse names: "activity room" (house 1), "billiard room" (house 10), "party room" (house 14). House 23 has a "living room" and a "children's living room"; houses 31 and 37 have large "playrooms."[23] Other interior rooms called "library," "den," "guest," and "study" suggest less social, more private uses. "Family room" is used to denote an informal social room in a few nineteenth-century house plans, but this is relatively rare until after World War II.[24] Then the emphasis on family togetherness encouraged the use of that term for a secondary living room, especially for children's games and activities. Family rooms adjacent to kitchens allowed the mother doing kitchen chores to always keep an eye on her kids. In 1940s and 1950s house plans, porches, decks, balconies, courtyards, terraces, and patios also offered outdoor social spaces.

While parlors and living rooms were ideally dedicated to sociability and family interactions, these rooms were appropriated for other uses when a house was too small. A Chicago man who had grown up in the 1930s in a three-bedroom bungalow described how his family found sleeping spaces for their six kids: "My brothers and I had our beds in the second parlor."[25]

The sociability of a living room could be shifted to the kitchen, especially in working-class dwellings. Families in working-class apartments and triple-deckers of post-World War II New England furnished their kitchens with comfortable upholstered chairs, typically in addition to the sink, the stove, and the refrigerator. The family would gather in the kitchen, converse, and assist with food preparation, making the kitchen essentially a living room.[26] Ann Hood's memoir of postwar life in an Italian community in Rhode Island described her mother's kitchen. She reports that the house was heated with a cast-iron coal stove standing in the middle of the kitchen; beside the stove was "a couch where we cuddled in winter—the warmest seat in the house."[27] She loved sitting there "listening as my mother and her five sisters talked, drinking coffee and smoking Pall Malls long into the night." Some of the family's other kitchen appliances were kept in the pantry, along with dishes, silverware, and cooking tools.

Recreation rooms stretched out the sociability zone of the house from its normal living room on the main floor in the post-World War II years. In his house-design handbook of 1853, Orson Squire Fowler had seen the need for a play space. His *Octagon House* design included a room called "Amusement" (room 28). This play space saw a surge in popularity in the 1940s and 1950s, reflecting new labor practices that gave workers more free time by limiting factory shifts to eight hours and preserving the weekend for leisure. Such rooms went by names such as "game room," "family play room," "entertainment room," and "rumpus room."

Developing an underused basement, garage, or attic into a recreation room, some homeowners installed an additional sink, refrigerator, and further food service conveniences. In these play spaces children could make noise without bothering their elders, but recreation rooms were also often sites for adult parties. One example is the "aloha bar" built in the basement of a one-story house in Hamburg, New York. The owner, returning from WWII military service in the South Pacific, installed a recreation room in his basement complete with near life-size painted images of hula girls and a bar with real seashells embedded in its surface. The columns that held up the ceiling were rendered as imitation palm trees, at the tops of which toy monkeys played. A less exotic recreation room for teenagers was advertised in 1956, promoting Armstrong tile. This basement room had a bar with stools, a couch, a coffee table, and a fireplace, and was rationalized as a way to save the living room upstairs for adult activities.

Fig. 27. In the mid-twentieth century, middle-class householders might finish off a basement room as a recreation space. Such a basement rec room amplified the house's social spaces expanding upon living rooms by providing special places for parties. Both the adults and their teenage children benefited by entertaining their friends in an easily cleaned space such as this one advertising Armstrong tile from 1956.

In the newer suburban areas of postwar Roseto, Pennsylvania—a town settled in the 1880s by Italian immigrants from Roseto, Italy—younger and wealthier residents moved into one-story houses with basements in the post–WWII era. The traditional street socializing that had characterized their parents' generation was discarded in favor of social life in basement rec rooms fitted up with a bar, sofas, and mirrors, and intended for adult parties. Whether for adults or teenagers, the 1950s basement rec room amplified the house's social spaces, expanding upon living rooms by assigning special places for parties.

Separating the kitchen from social space had remained a goal for homeowners, builders, and designers for much of the eighteenth, nineteenth, and early twentieth centuries, but modern architects of the 1940s and 1950s began to explore open plans where the spaces of previously isolated kitchens were joined to living rooms and dining rooms as one flowing unit. Since the early years of the twentieth century, servant labor for the prosperous classes was increasingly hard to come by, leaving all but the

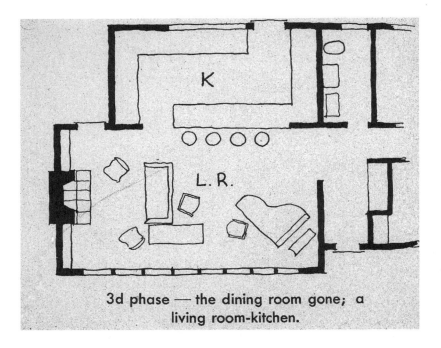

3d phase — the dining room gone; a living room-kitchen.

Fig. 28. Modern architects in the 1940s began to use an open plan for social space that removed the limits of formerly individual rooms including kitchens, allowing them to flow together. Architect Royal Barry Wills published his book *Living on the Level* in 1955, advising house-builders or renovators to take down the walls and blend formerly separate rooms into one. Royal Barry Wills, *Living on the Level* (Boston: Houghton Mifflin, 1955).

wealthiest housewives to do that service work themselves. Housewives resisted isolation, preferring to do their work in sight of their children, partners, and guests, not hidden away like a servant in an enclosed kitchen. Popular magazines published advice to help homeowners tear down ground-floor walls and open up kitchens to previously contained and specialized dining rooms and living rooms. The boundaries of the mid-twentieth-century middle-class living room began to dissolve with the increasing informality of post–WWII life.[29]

"Living-kitchen" is the name of the newly informal social centerpiece of a 1945 house published in *Architectural Forum*.[30] This design jettisons the idea of unrelated separate rooms and "instead divides the house according to use"—use defined by noisy activities or quiet activities. The noisy area is the living-kitchen, "where the entire family spends most of its waking hours." The proposed quiet area includes bedrooms, a study, and perhaps even a second living room. In the noisy family zone, cooking, dining, and laundry/sewing areas are demarcated by cabinets acting as semi-partitions. The dining area can be enlarged with sliding glass doors onto a screened porch where twenty to thirty people may be entertained. The "noisy" zone of this house includes kitchen and laundry, which historically were closed off in a service zone. By the 1940s the housewife, and not a maid, is the occupant of the service zone, so those functions get incorporated into the

Fig. 29. The "Living-Kitchen" by architect Almon Fordyce fused the sociability of the living room and dining room with the warmth and domestic comfort of the kitchen. Modern open planning enabled views from area to area just as it enabled views out of the house through picture windows. *Architectural Forum* (May 1945): 107–12.

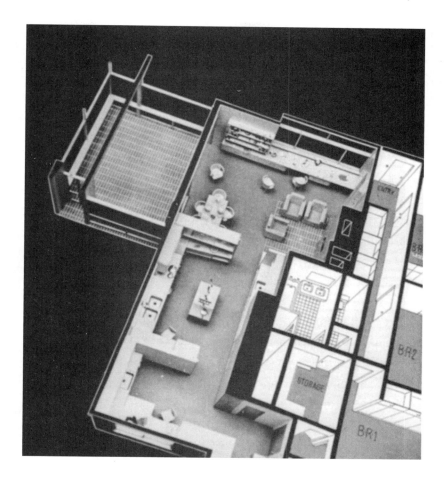

social space. From the point of view of visitors, the "living room" is made up of the living-dining-screened porch sequence. They would catch a glimpse of the open kitchen and utility spaces, but wouldn't use them.

The newly visible kitchen was a beneficiary of several technological improvements. Better-working electric refrigerators, continuous-countertop kitchen cabinets, washable linoleum flooring, and reliable plumbing all contributed to a kitchen that was cleaner and did smell better than its nineteenth-century counterpart. This kitchen's success as a social space was also due to the efforts of the postwar-era housewife. She was continually reminded by advertisements and magazine articles to have high standards of cleanliness and to devote her days to home maintenance.[31]

The Kitchen as Social Space

In the last forty years of the twentieth century in new construction, the expanded great-room kitchen unexpectedly took on the role that living rooms had previously filled. One of the smallest rooms for home economists in the 1910s following scientific efficiency studies, kitchens in the 1980s now became one of the largest rooms, incorporating the family room, sometimes renamed "great room," and outfitted with dining and living room furniture, television, a computer, and equipment for other leisure activities. Kitchens acquired upholstered seating furniture like that found in living rooms. In the 1980s and 1990s in expensive dwellings, some expanded kitchens turned theater-like as guests were entertained with cooking events and appliances grew to restaurant proportions and quality.

Existing houses were expanded with rear additions of "great rooms," high-ceilinged family-room-kitchen combinations where a crowd of family or guests could gather. Fireplaces, once expected in living rooms, were constructed in the new kitchens—sentimentally associated with idealized "farm kitchens" of the eighteenth and nineteenth centuries. In receptive climates well-to-do homeowners built duplicate outdoor kitchens for entertaining on the deck or patio. The popular kitchen of the past forty years reversed the home economists' theories and incorporated social space back into the kitchen, while attempting to preserve an efficient work zone in the newly enlarged, multi-purpose room.

"Today's kitchen is the social center of the home," said an advertisement for Sears Kenmore appliances in a 1999 issue of *Bon Appetit*; "the place to cook, entertain and relax with friends and family."[32] Architect Brad Walker called the kitchen "the new living room" and pointed out that some new houses dispense with living rooms altogether.[33] While there is still a space called kitchen, many houses have lost their dining rooms and many other rooms have acquired aspects of the kitchen: appliances in ever smaller renditions can be located in any room of the house, dissolving the clear boundaries among functions seen in middle-class houses of the nineteenth and early twentieth centuries. This blurring of boundaries accompanied an overall increase in average house size in the United States. In 1970 the average house had fifteen hundred square feet, while in 2018 it had grown to twenty-four hundred.[34]

While middle-class residents would be surprised at the parallels, working-class tenement dwellers would recognize the "heart-of-the-home" kitchen as a good description of their own earlier practices. The new great-room kitchen is much closer to the working-class tenement living room with its merged functions. The largest tenement room, usually called "living room," contained the stove, a table, chairs, and sometimes beds, and served

Spruce Lake 1,825 sq

DECK

KITCHEN DINING AREA BATH MASTER BEDROOM

32'-3"

LIVING ROOM

BEDROOM BEDROOM

50'-11"

FIRST FLOOR

Fig. 30. Living-dining-room-kitchen. An open-plan living-eating-cooking space became popular with developers for middle-class houses in the 1960s and later. This plan shows the continuous space resulting from breaking down dividing walls. While owners appreciated the openness, those with noisy children also felt the loss of rooms whose doors could be shut. Spruce Lake model house from Timberhaven Log and Timber Homes brochure, *Modern Log Houses* (PA: 1995).

as the cooking and eating room as well as the room for income-producing work and sleeping. This living room operated like the seventeenth-century hall with its combined functions and presaged the late twentieth-century great-room kitchen that upper-middle-class homeowners came to prefer. It is not the case that recent designers were looking at tenement living rooms for ideas, but that in striving to lead modern lives, middle-class thinkers repudiated the formal manners and strict room uses that their Victorian forebears had insisted on. Once those manners, tools to differentiate the middle class from the working class, were outgrown, the new middle-class spaces for informal socializing and family interactions came to resemble the openness and mutifunctionality of tenement living rooms, albeit in greatly expanded square footage.

Materials themselves convey associations with social rooms. The associations of comfort and relaxation tied to an informal living room turn up in the décor and fittings of the new social kitchen.[35] Designer Sandra Nunnerly avoided what she called the old-fashioned streamlined aesthetic of modernist kitchens and instead disguised kitchen hardware with lots of woodwork to produce "sitting-room elegance."[36] Annemarie and Michael Garstin's Sag Harbor, New York kitchen has limestone floors echoing their entrance hall, as well as sophisticated cornices and paneling for "an elegantly inviting ambience." Judy Baum's Sub-Zero refrigerator is disguised behind "hand-carved mahogany panels" in her Sanibel, Florida kitchen; she wants it to look like a French armoire.[37] In small apartments where the kitchen becomes part of the general living space and may be the room you first enter upon opening the front door, it is increasingly common to find reception-room materials such fine woods, granite, and quartz, as well as atmospheric lighting.

Social spaces became more specific and dedicated in formal eras, and more diverse in houses where informal manners prevailed.[38] In each era it is characteristic to furnish the socializing room with best-quality materials and furnishings both to provide comfort for guests and to impress them. Those of the eighteenth century whose prosperity allowed them to build grander houses focused their decorating on social rooms—parlors and dining rooms—enriched by architectural columns and moldings, decorative carvings, or wallpapers. Victorian parlors furnished with rarely used suites of elaborate furniture may have seemed to family members too precious to use. Later living rooms attempted to create a sense of comfort where all ages could enjoy themselves. Contrary to early twentieth-century home economists who urged the smallest, most efficient kitchen that excluded all but the cook, contemporary living-kitchens include everyone. The modern living-kitchen can achieve efficiency in its food preparation zone with electric and digital appliances rather than by the compact spatial arrangements required in the 1910s.

3
SPACES FOR EATING

While everyone eats, American houses have had very different spaces to accommodate the serving of meals.[1] There are changing fashions in how meals are popularly served, different attitudes toward meals at diverse income levels or ethnic backgrounds, and regional preferences in how residents and guests are treated around food service. Early New England families served meals in several rooms of their houses, using finer implements and furnishings to celebrate higher status guests and important occasions. Plantation owners in eighteenth-century Virginia rebuilt older parlors into grand dining rooms, making them the largest rooms in the house. The enslaved families that served them often had no tables or chairs in their dwellings but simply ate whenever they found some food. Victorian strivers aimed to present good manners in a dedicated dining room with proper china and matching suites of furniture, while less prosperous middling households might be able to afford only a nice tea set to signal their class aspirations. Frugal workers in early twentieth-century bungalows served meals in their kitchens on built-in tables and benches. And many over-committed twenty-first-century families eat some meals in their cars.

The overall direction of dining-room development until the early twentieth century tended toward focusing the room increasingly on furnishings and equipment for food service. Then, alternatives to dining rooms entered into houses at all levels—small houses because owners couldn't afford the extra square footage, and larger houses because owners suspected that dining rooms were wasted space or too formal. Historically dining had been a focused activity in a clearly purposed room, but in recent decades it has become more diffuse and distributed in the house and the room itself has taken in more diverse activities.

Seventeenth- and Eighteenth-Century Dining Practices

The notion that meals should be served to individuals is one of the markers of difference between medieval and modern sensibilities. In medieval forms of eating people used their fingers instead of forks and shared drinking vessels and common platters of food much as we might share a pizza today. Archaeological and inventory research shows that in seventeenth-century Maine people ate with their fingers and used communal drinking vessels, preserving a medieval practice. Soups, stews, and other mixtures of meat and vegetables on one platter were eaten with fingers, or with the aid of knives and spoons, but no forks. In Massachusetts at the same time, however, many households had wooden trenchers—planks or plates—on which to serve individual portions of food.[2] These regional distinctions also had an economic dimension. In the Chesapeake region, archaeologists have found scant ceramic wares but plenty of pewter, suggesting that individuals could eat from their own plates in established households that possessed pewter saucers, plates, and bowls in addition to wooden vessels for food.[3] Poor people continued the tradition of eating stews out of a communal pot well into the nineteenth century.

It is always surprising to note which eating equipment belongs to, or should be found in, a house at a particular moment and what belongs elsewhere. When seventeenth-century travelers owned eating implements, they took their knives and forks with them.[4] In 1679 European missionary Jasper Danckaerts and his comrade were traveling in Maryland, finding a bed at the homes of various people who lived along their route and offered them hospitality for the night.[5] Having left their host's home and traveled on the road for two hours, they were upset to discover that they had left a knife and fork behind at the last house they had stayed in. That the travelers had to carry their own knives and forks suggests that homeowners either did not use them themselves or did not have enough implements for guests. Today we would be amazed to find ourselves in an American house that was not supplied with knives and forks, plates and cups, tables and chairs; but we would bring our own clothing, cell phones, and toiletries.

The gesture of separating eating in a dining room from cooking in a kitchen was a significant step in establishing the gentility of a household. Messy workspaces on the food axis—the collection of all the food-related spaces—could then be secured as behind-the-scenes private areas, while

Fig. 31. The Randolph family's Virginia house, Tuckahoe, was expanded in 1740 to acquire a dedicated dining room. Guests at ambitiously prepared meals would enjoy the decorative details of the dining room, and then—using it as a sitting room—linger after the meal for conversation. Drawing by Camille Wells.

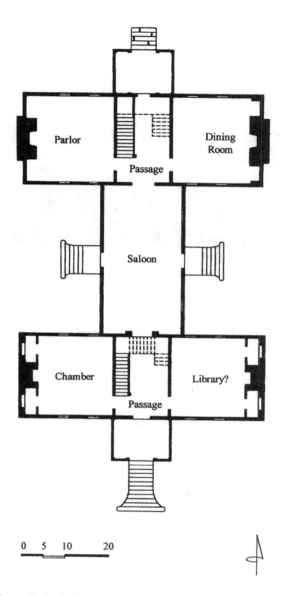

the polished dining room represented cleanliness, elegance, and public display. References to dining rooms in American inventories occur as early as the seventeenth century—architectural historian Abbot Cummings quotes a New England inventory from 1669 that mentions a separate "dyning Roome."[6] Merchant Edmund Downes's 1669 inventory named a hall, two parlors, a kitchen and a dining room in his five-hearth main floor. Benjamin Gibbs's 1678 inventory listed a great hall, a dining room, and two other unnamed main-floor rooms.[7] But normally seventeenth-century people ate their meals in the hall, the parlor, or one of the chambers—not in a dedicated dining room.

The Randolph family managed the expansion of their food spaces as they improved their house called Tuckahoe, begun in 1733 in Goochland County, Virginia. The main floor had two large rooms—a chamber and a hall—located on either side of a central passage containing a staircase going up to the chamber floor. According to historian Camille Wells's analysis, the hall was originally the place the Randolphs used for dining. Dining rooms had not yet become separate, dedicated rooms for most of the Virginia gentry in the 1730s, so Tuckahoe's hall would have functioned both as "a formal sitting room and as a place for taking meals."[8] The room had finely finished paneled walls with pilasters and a cornice. Built-in cabinets stored china, pewter, and silver objects. Wealthy families of this period possessed the equipment for fine dining and the desire to entertain friends and family, but had yet to define these activities as requiring a dedicated room for meals.

By 1740, William and Maria Randolph added a hyphen or linking space and a wing to Tuckahoe in order to create more entertaining spaces. The original two rooms, Wells explains, were redecorated and renamed *parlor* and *dining room*. The linking space between the original house and the new wing was designated "saloon" and used for entertainments. In the new wing, the Randolphs created a new chamber for themselves, an additional passage, and a staircase to the second floor, and another public room that could be used as a secondary dining room, a sitting room, or another bedroom. Now the family had one dedicated dining room for their own and their guests' meals, plus a second room sometimes used as a dining room.[9]

The Warner House in Portsmouth, New Hampshire, completed in 1723, has a dining room given a very public location—it was entered by a door opening from the entrance hall and just left of the front door. The Warner House dining room has a direct connection to the kitchen to make food service more fluid as well as a windowed pantry-like closet between the kitchen and dining room that hints of later butler's pantry spaces. In the years approaching the middle of the eighteenth century, then, formal dining rooms, called by that name in inventories of the period, entered the list of expected rooms in a well-to-do household. In mid-eighteenth-century Virginia, dining rooms became ever more important for entertaining. The owners of the Nelson House started with a decorated parlor and a small dining room, and when dining rooms gained more importance, they took the smaller room for their parlor and the largest room for dining. They enhanced the dining room with classical pilasters and moldings.

The wealthiest families could afford to create a dining room just for dining, but those of lesser incomes used their dining-room space in less cleanly defined ways. Observing the introduction of the term "dining room" into middling Virginia householders' inventories, historian Dell Upton found that this room name emerged in the second quarter of the eighteenth century and became quite popular by the third quarter. However the earliest dining rooms still contained anomalous objects: "In 1727 Mr. Christopher Robinson's dining room contained, besides ten chairs and an old table, two bedsteads."[10] So, while dining may have happened in rooms called "dining rooms," so did many other activities and the storage of unrelated tools. When householders first began to add rooms called "dining room," they frequently contained mixed equipment and diverse uses. Rooms for dining did not have the degree of functional specificity that dairies or smoke houses did; one could always use a dining room for storage, sitting, sleeping, or other unspecified uses, as people had used their early halls for cooking plus all sorts of other activities.

What Upton finds more significant is that the room called "dining room" was inserted into the circulation path of the house to stretch the distance between a public entrance and busy hall and the owners' private chamber. The addition of this dining room seems to have been motivated by the need to better secure privacy and control access to the owners' chamber rather than by the need for a room in which to dine. Interestingly, later nineteenth- and early twentieth-century dining rooms in middle-class houses also commonly served the purpose of a circulation element, making that room less private, more subject to interruption. Perhaps because of predictable traffic through the dining room, it has usually served multiple purposes in addition to dining.

Typical uses of dining spaces in the Chesapeake region are illuminated by Philip Fithian's diary. He was a tutor to the Carter children and lived at the Carter home, Nomini Hall, Virginia, in the 1770s. Nomini Hall had four rooms per floor: on the main floor is first the "dining room where we usually sit; the second is a dining room for the Children; the third is Mr. Carter's study; & the fourth is a Ball-Room thirty feet long." The upper floor had sleeping rooms. Describing his day, Philip reported that he taught early, then went to the dining room for breakfast from 8:30 to 9:30. At about 2:00 or 2:30 p.m. he returned to the dining room where dinner was served, followed by a supper at 8:30 or 9:00 p.m. One night, he said, the dining room "looked luminous and splendid" with four large candles on the supper table and three others in different parts of the room.[11]

On the lower rungs of society dining was much less formal, and in cities, small towns, and rural and farm settings, small houses did not allow the elaboration of specific rooms for dining. Small houses of one room with a loft above were very common for artisans in the eighteenth century. The Baltimore house built for Angus and Jane Grant measured twelve by sixteen feet—192 square feet of living space plus the loft above. Furniture for every use filled the one room: a bedstead, three tables, three chairs, fireplace and kitchen equipment, his joiner's tools, a tea caddy, and a tea tray.[12] The niceties of dining, seen in the tea equipment, were familiar to these artisans, but they simply could not afford to give them more space. A French traveler in late eighteenth-century New England was distressed to discover the lack of aristocratic rank in the dining arrangements. "The masters, mistresses, and servants generally eat at the same table it generally happening that the latter are composed of neighbors' children or relations who look upon themselves as fully equal to their employers."[13]

Nineteenth-Century Dining Rooms

In elite households the dining room retained its primary function as a social space. An example is the Gibson House, a row house in the Back Bay area of Boston, Massachusetts. Built in the late 1850s, the Gibson House had a spacious entrance hall with an imposing staircase, and a dining room at the rear directly on axis with the front door. This dining room was the first room visitors could see, finely decorated with elaborate moldings, an ornate fireplace, a bay window, and paintings. Adjacent to the dining room and concealed by a decorative screen were the associated pantry and a dumbwaiter linking the dining room to the basement kitchen. Below, kitchen servants prepared food; their work space was expanded by a rear yard with a woodshed and a privy. Many prosperous households adopted this arrangement with dining above and kitchen below, connected by a dumbwaiter, service stairs, and a butler's pantry—a system supporting meal service. Middling families, wanting visitors to first see their parlor, located both kitchen and dining room in urban basements. Rear service doors linked these basements with deliveries and trash disposal managed in service alleys and backyards.[14]

Many households used images of nature to decorate dining rooms, such as pictures of birds or animals and even stuffed animal heads. Both live and dried plants were also popular in conveying the link between dining and nature. Even lighting fixtures were made in natural forms such as the 1890s sculpted deer heads holding glass light shades in their mouths, made by

Fig. 32. Mary Northend, a colonial-revival photographer, recorded this dining room showing nature themes in its decoration. Nature motifs commonly provided elements of dining-room décor: they referred to nature's bounty, the source of the meal to be served. Photo courtesy of Historic New England.

Gibson Gas Fixture Works in Philadelphia.[15] Such references to nature were popular because the food to be consumed in the dining room was itself a bounty of nature. Nature features in the decoration at the Mavis house in Buffalo, New York, where the dining room is dominated by an enormous taxidermied head.[16]

Not only is food the product of nature, but eating food brings to the fore the body's animal nature—its digestive processes, sounds, and smells. Proper Victorian manners reminded diners that they should eat silently, touch their food as little as possible, and avoid commenting on the food. Paying too much attention to the food would give expression to "'animal and sensual gratification' over mankind's 'intellect . . . and . . . moral nature.'"[17] In a diatribe against the entertainment function of the dining room, architect Ralph Adams Cram lamented that his contemporaries liked to entertain their friends by eating meals with them. He protested that eating was only an animal activity, and that the host and hostess may as well invite their friends to sleep together as to eat together.

In lower-budget houses it was and still is common to have cooking and serving meals occupy the same room. Oliver B. Smith's 1854 pattern book *The Domestic Architect* promoted designs for small cottages and farm houses. His small cottage, house XXXIII, described as "very conveniently arranged," shows the elements of cooking and eating condensed in the kitchen. On the ground floor a kitchen at fourteen by sixteen feet has a windowed pantry for storage. There is no dining room.

At the same time that mid-nineteenth-century upper-middle-class homeowners were elaborating their dining rooms, homesteaders built simpler houses for themselves. The federal Homestead Act of 1862 allowed each settler household to claim 160 acres if they occupied it continuously for five years. Americans moved from established settlements on the Eastern Seaboard and elsewhere. Unlike seventeenth-century newcomers, however, these householders were acquainted with the new conveniences that industry produced and often were able to acquire one or two elements of the modern food axis in spite of their rustic circumstances.

In the straightened circumstances of the frontier, houses had too little space to set aside a room just for dining. Fortescue Cuming, a traveler walking west from Harrisburg, Pennsylvania in the early nineteenth century, stopped at a Mr. Ramsey's log house, staying for three days. Cuming was invited to sit at the table for a meal. He observed at the center of one room a calico-covered "dining table" and four chairs with woven hickory seats, plus two stools and a bench. Nailed to one side wall, some boards made the equivalent of a storage unit. Tableware comprised a few tin cups, a few trenchers—pieces of wood to serve as plates— and a candlestick made from a corn cob.[18]

It seems from this description that the Ramseys had arranged to make a dining room, but without the functional purity that a well-to-do household

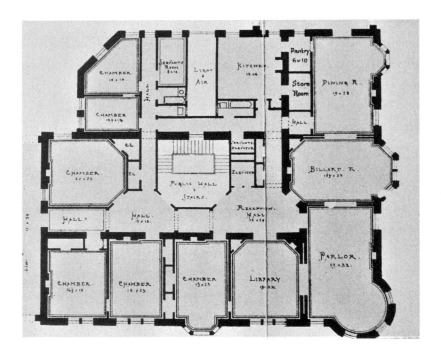

Fig. 33. Plan of the 1883 Central Park Apartments. A dining room, part of the socializing part of the house, was located along a string of social rooms that could be opened to each other for parties. It was also placed near the kitchen so maids could easily serve meals. *The Central Park Apartments*, 1882 pamphlet (New York Public Library collection).

Fig. 34. A maid serves nine—two children and seven adults—at the dining room table. In the eighteenth and nineteenth centuries, even middling families had some household help. But when factory jobs offered better wages than household work, the servant labor force aimed higher. Illustration from *The Social Mirror* (St. Louis: 1888), 178.

would demand. Fortescue Cuming recorded that one corner of the room was full of hoes, axes, flails, and wooden forks for agriculture. From the ceiling hung herbs for medicines, smoked meats, and two guns. The room in which they were dining also contained a bed; four large pots of honey occupied the space under it.[19] Like the eighteenth-century Virginia houses that Upton investigated in which middling families first set aside a "dining room," the Ramseys' room that was used for dining was also used for sleeping, drying herbs, and storing smoked meats, honey, tools, and guns. Special arrangements for dining—be it separate rooms, fine decorations, careful manners, or elaborate equipment—belonged to the more prosperous in this era, while others got along with less ceremony in their meal spaces.

African American scholar Booker T. Washington recalled his childhood "dining" experiences in the 1860s.[20] He could not remember the family ever sitting down at the table together: "Meals were gotten by the children very much as dumb animals get theirs. It was a piece of bread here and a scrap of meat there." Some would eat from the skillet or pot, some from the tin plate on their knees; they had no knives and forks to eat with, just their hands. Their house had no dining room nor dining table.

One-floor urban dwellings posed problems of organization to architects accustomed to multi-floor houses for the well-to-do. In order to maintain the good manners that prescribed separating smelly cooking from elegant dining, the dining rooms in apartments were grouped with the other

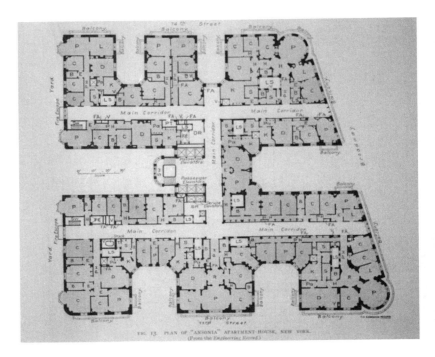

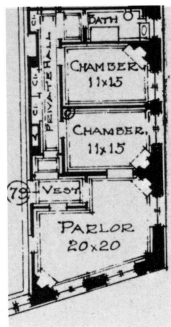

reception rooms like parlors and libraries, and separated from cooking. Apartment house design matured through the 1870s and 1880s, as designers tried to bring kitchens and dining rooms into closer proximity to each other for more convenient food service.

At the Central Park Apartments of 1884, the architects Hubert, Pirsson, and Hoddick designed large family apartments. They located the dining room at the end of a string of reception rooms that could be opened to each other for grand parties. Adjacent to the dining room were a kitchen and pantries ventilated to a rear courtyard; these rooms were a few steps up or down from the reception rooms and had lower ceilings. Thus the kitchen had the requisite proximity to dining, but it still sequestered labor and smells from the dining experience. In smaller apartment houses where the individual units had smaller square footage, designers tried to zone groups of functional rooms but could not always achieve the separation between zones that they would have liked.

Another way to create dining space for prosperous families in an apartment house or hotel was to provide both a central hotel-like dining room and restaurant kitchen as well as private kitchens and dining rooms in some of the units. The Ansonia Apartment-Hotel units varied in size from a kitchenless two- or three-room unit for bachelors to a multi-bedroom family

Fig. 35a and Fig. 35b. Floor plan of the Ansonia Apartment-Hotel and one of its kitchenless apartments in New York. Since the tenants were served by a central kitchen and restaurant-like dining room run by the building management, they did not need a kitchen. Residents could reserve a table in the central dining room, or request that dinner, prepared in the central kitchen, be sent to their individual unit. The units varied in size from a kitchenless two-room for bachelors to a multi-bedroom unit with its own fully equipped kitchen and dining room for those who preferred to prepare their own meals. *American Architect and Building News* 91 (January 5, 1907): 7.

unit with fully equipped kitchen and dining room. Residents could cook in their own kitchens, or reserve a table in the central dining room, or request that dinner, prepared in the central kitchen, be sent to their individual unit.

Efficient Dining Concepts for the Twentieth Century

In the early twentieth century, an era of efficiency in which arts-and-crafts simplicity was the favorite style of many, built-in dining room furniture provided a way to expand stylish design features. For home economists such as Isabelle Bevier, built-in storage units helped a housewife run her house by herself without the aid of servants while creating economies in the purchase of furniture. Dining rooms suggested themselves as likely sites for "built-in furniture," according to a 1913 *House and Garden* article, in contrast to the living room where "movable pieces of furniture seem rather more appropriate."[21] A built-in china closet affords more space than the average movable china closet, is less conspicuous, and can be made artistic: "A handsome sideboard of mahogany or oak is preferred to the built-in variety, but if there are limitations on floor space or budget, a built-in sideboard can work very well, not least because you can plan adequate space for your silver and table linens, not always provided in movable pieces, and also because it can be made to match woodwork." China closets can be built in on either side of the chimney piece and make useful additions even to a dining room that has plenty of room for movable pieces.[22] Bungalow builders found it practical to include built-in furniture—buffets, china closets, writing desks, even beds—which suited the customer who wanted to save on housekeeping and furnishing. Especially in southern California, said *House and Garden's* 1913 author, the customer was often a winter resident, a transient, or a man of small means.

Even though dining rooms could be made efficient with built-in furniture and reduced square footage, critics began to identify the dining room as a wasted space. Since the family gathered for a meal only two or three times a day, surely a way could be found to make better use of the space in a house; designers should make sure that a room was usable all day long. In a 1927 article called "Abolish the Dining Room" in *Collier's*, the author, Edward W. Bok, argued that dining rooms were unnecessary and old-fashioned. Why spend the extra money for space that is so little used? Modern families would prefer to use one end of the living room for dining, Bok argued, where the china and linens could be stored in built-in cabinets. Once dining

Fig. 36. Critics of dining rooms argued that they were only used a couple of hours a day and therefore were a big waste of space and money. Better to set aside one end of the living room where one could keep a table and chairs for dining. Linens and china could easily be concealed in a nearby closet. When it is time for dinner, set the table and bring in the meal. After the dishes are cleared, turn the area back into a living room. Edward Bok, "Abolish the Dining Room," *Colliers* 79 (January 15, 1927): 10.

materials were put away, the living room could return to its sociable uses, and the family could save on square footage by not incorporating a separate dining room in their house. Just as no old-fashioned "parlor" would today be included in a new middle-class house, wrote Bok, so too the dining room as we know it will soon disappear.[23] A table, set and concealed by a screen until dinner is served, makes the use of the living room for dining perfectly feasible. Omitting the dining room gives the housewife one less room to furnish and clean, and might in some cases mean one fewer maid. "We forget that the parlor and dining-room were handed down to us from the drawing-room and dining-room of feudal times, forgetting that these rooms are no longer necessary in our time," wrote Bok.[24]

It is practical to combine dining and kitchen functions, said a 1905 *Craftsman* magazine article, in households where no servants are kept. While an expensive house could have both a dining room and a breakfast room, at the lower-income end the separation of dining from cooking might only take place in a little built-in nook at one end of the kitchen. Building in a table and benches, either foldable ones or those permanently in place, allowed houses at the least expensive end of the market to provide specialized dining settings for their owners at one end of the kitchen. The *Craftsman* author argued that the pots and pans hanging in the kitchen could be just as ornamental as racks of plates on display in formal dining rooms.[25] A recess at one end of a kitchen "may well serve as a most comfortable and homelike dining room," because modern kitchen appliances and plumbing are so easy to keep clean.

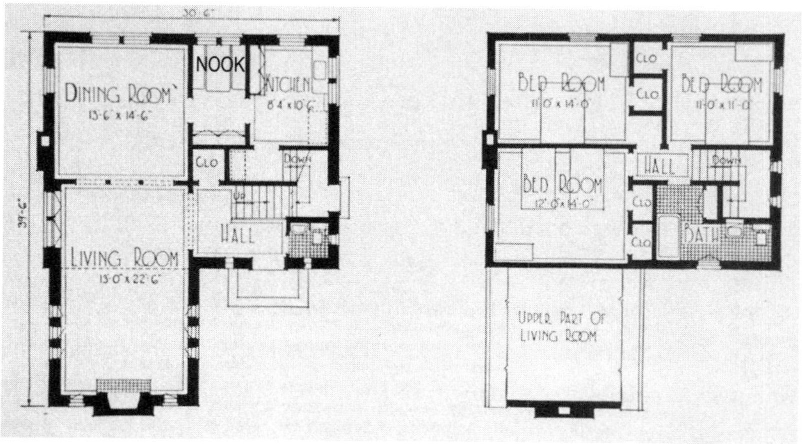

Fig. 37. Inexpensive houses where there was no room for separate dining rooms nonetheless provided dedicated eating space. Working-class householders often located eating space at the end of the kitchen. Plan of built-in nook: house by architect Charles E. White, 1923, in *500 Small Houses of the Twenties* (repr., Dover: 1990), 146.

Fig. 38. Modest dwelling in Greenbelt, Maryland. Designers planned for a dining table and chairs in the living room. 1939. Photo E. C. Cromley.

Sears Roebuck house kits of the 1920s provided living rooms that were also to serve for dining, and diagrams in the catalog showed how to furnish these rooms. In their house model, "The Valley," for example, the room is presented with a round table and four chairs supporting the dining function, while two side chairs and a piano (no room for a "davenport" or sofa) represented the living room's social function.[26]

A 1924 issue of *American Builder* showed a built-in table and two benches creating a breakfast nook in a house that also had a dining room. Instructions for building such a nook were given in William A. Radford's *Architectural Details* of 1921, in which he gave dimensions of the various parts of the table and benches and explained how to locate the nook at the end of the kitchen adjacent to the dining-room door.[27] *New York Times* writer Rick Marin recalled in 2006, "I grew up in a house with a sunny, closed kitchen whose small corner booth was upholstered in turquoise vinyl . . . I spent countless hours in that booth." He wanted to replicate "the same familial coziness" when he constructed a new built-in nook in his family's 2006 house.[28]

The magazine *American Builder* published an illustration of what they called a Pulmanook in 1924. It consisted of a table to be stored against the wall with an end leg that folded up underneath it, and seats beside the table which pulled out from indentations in the wall. Their illustrations show the

Fig. 39. A counter with stools provides many families with an informal place to eat at the edge of the kitchen. The Schultz family modernized their kitchen in the 1970s with knotty-pine surfaces, widening the kitchen counter for eating space. Renovated nineteenth-century main house at the Z-Bar Ranch in Washington, Kansas. Photo E. C. Cromley.

Pulmanook installed in a narrow bay of space with four pull-down seats—two on each side—or alternatively installed in the corner of the kitchen with two pull-down seats mounted in the wall and a movable chair for supplementary seating. This kind of fold-up furniture recalls early eighteenth-century expedients such as tip-up beds. Another common postwar way to include eating space in the kitchen is to expand the width of a kitchen counter, making room for stools beneath it and enabling family members to pull up a stool to eat informal meals.

A less working-class arrangement was to combine living room and dining room functions. In a 1901 *Ladies' Home Journal* essay, architect Frank Lloyd Wright had suggested making the dining room "a sunny alcove of the living room," a very unusual arrangement for this date and for his then servant-run houses.[29] Following his own advice, Wright merged living room with dining room space in his own house, the 1911 Taliesin East.

After World War II thousands of new single-family houses were built around the United States. The food axis in a house of this sort was contained in the kitchen and wherever the family chose to eat its meals. Returning service members were eligible to get government-subsidized mortgages, which they used to buy their first houses. Such houses were often ranch or cape styles and fairly small. Householders could have squeezed a table into the small kitchen, installed a built-in dinette table and benches, or had a table at one end of the living room. Mrs. Eckhoff, a Levittown resident interviewed for *McCall's* magazine, said that she kept both a small center table with two chairs in the kitchen and another table and chairs in the living room, both of which served for dining.[30] One woman reported that her 1961 house had a too-small dining area as an extension of the kitchen, so when "we had people in, we had to set up tables in the living room."[31]

Although small, the 1940s, four-room, cape-style Levittown house allowed numerous people to get a foothold in the housing market. In 1949, Levitt started building a ranch house design—this time for purchase, not rental. It still offered four rooms, but the kitchen was at the front and the main entrance opened directly into it. The ranch house included a fireplace that acted as the divider between the kitchen and the living room, to create a more open flow of space as well as reinforcing the kitchen as the center of home life. By 1957, ten years after the Long Island Levittown was first occupied, people had renovated their houses. Once Levittowners had more resources, they wanted the five-room standard with a separate dining room and created it for themselves.[32] The most common decision was to add a

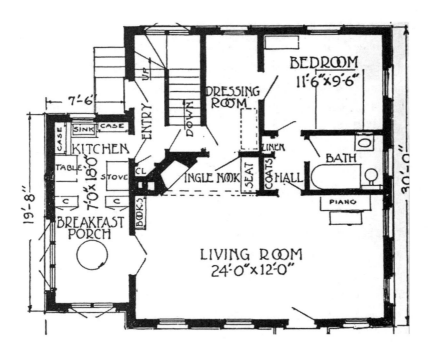

Fig. 40. Plan of an inexpensive house from the 1920s shows how combining dining with the kitchen gives each function enough room while maximizing spatial economy. This type of plan, here combining "breakfast porch" with kitchen, was also common for apartments. *500 Small Houses of the Twenties* (repr., Dover, NY: 1990), 12. First published 1923 as *The Books of a Thousand Homes*, ed. Henry Atterbury Smith.

room to the rear; that became a living room, allowing the old living room to become a dining room.

In order to remedy living conditions for working-class families, publicly subsidized multi-family housing was built in major cities during the 1940s. In New York City a large project called East River houses, completed in 1941, constituted the first public housing project of high-rise buildings in New York. An apartment at the East River houses offered a fully applianced kitchen, seven by seven foot four, adjacent to the dining area, seven foot three by eight foot three, at the right of the apartment entrance. To the left of the entrance was a living room, while two bedrooms and a bathroom to the rear completed the plan.[33] This apartment had two dedicated spaces, one for cooking and one for eating, but this was hardly the dining room of earlier times, since the two spaces were very small and open to each other. The food zone in this housing for lower-income households adopted the efficient layouts familiar from economical middle-class bungalows in the 1910s with even tighter dimensions. The small square footages of these rooms was made workable by modern appliances that were widely available after the war. While the kitchen and dining area for lower-income tenants had fewer square feet than the same spaces in various middle-class examples, providing an efficient kitchen with modern appliances and a dedicated dining room was still a goal for subsidized apartment housing.

Having a separate dining room did make it possible to adapt that room to other purposes; in fact, dining rooms could double as bedrooms when necessary. A report from a Chicago woman told of living with her husband in an apartment in 1956 that was too small for the couple and their two children: "Lou and I had to sleep in the dining room."[34] When her husband Lou was a boy, his mother along with seven other family members rented a two-bedroom house, "so some of them slept in the dining room and some in the living-room on a hide-a-bed."

Dining Interpretations by Modern Architects

Architect-designed modern houses for wealthier households used the need for dining space as an excuse to experiment. Multiple places to eat were featured in the 1940 "House of Glass" by Landefeld and Hatch, described by author Otto Teegan as "extremely modern."[35] The House of Glass family could choose to eat a meal in the breakfast nook, the dining room proper, or the patio, expanding upon the choices that would have been available a few decades earlier. There is a built-in breakfast nook with benches and a table, linked to the kitchen. There is a dining room, separable from the other living spaces by means of sliding walls. The dining space also opens onto an outdoor patio with another table and chairs. A proper family of the 1890s would have had neither the breakfast nook nor the patio, but would have taken their meals only in the dining room.

Instead of abolishing the dining room by utilizing one end of the living room, architect Raymond Hood abolished it as an indoor space by relocating the dining function to outdoors. Hood's 1933 "Forward House" design stressed the use of outdoor space for living; he believed that in most regions of the United States outdoor living was comfortable up to seven months of the year. His house was organized around a south-facing, masonry-walled dining porch, heated by a fireplace, and neither glazed nor screened. Kitchen and living room opened onto this porch, saving steps for "the housewife or the maid." Presumably during the five months in which outdoor living is not so pleasant in the chillier parts of the country, one would still use the end of the living room for dining functions.

Architect Royal Barry Wills equated having separate rooms with having an old-fashioned house in his 1955 book, *Living on the Level* (see fig. 28). Instead of the old segregated social and service zones, he recommended an open living-dining-kitchen space.[36] Wills believed that counters, screens,

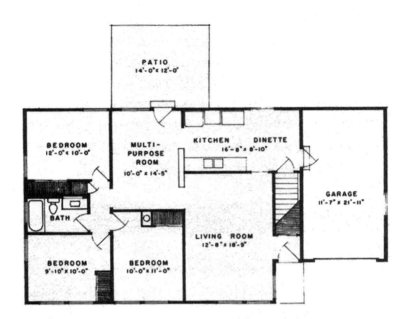

Fig. 41. Middle-class house of 1959 by Pearce Developers of Buffalo, New York, with a living room, multi-purpose room, dinette, and kitchen grouped together and accessible to each other through wide openings. *Pearce and Pearce Parade of Homes* booklet, 1959.

and "room-divider" furniture would replace the containing walls that had segregated earlier domestic spaces. This attitude is a reversal of the one Edward Bok had expressed in his campaign to eliminate the 1920s dining room. Then he took care to conceal the dining function in the living room, finding it an embarrassment to have a multi-purpose living room.[37] Instead, Wills's open plan prefigures the loft apartments as well as suburban houses that became popular in many regions in the 1970s through the 1990s.

Merging living and dining functions was promoted by popular shelter magazines such as *Better Homes and Gardens*, which published the Mack family's "den-dining room" in 1947. They had taken down the wall of their California house that bounded their kitchen nook and joined the space to a too-small den; half-doors opened into the kitchen for "easy service."[38] The resulting pine-paneled room was furnished with a built-in round table and circular seat, a piano, a couch, and bookshelves. In the 1940s and 1950s, a variety of strategies for merging service and reception activities could be found at all levels of the middle class.

The elimination of dining rooms in more expensive houses of the late twentieth century might remind us of working-class examples, but it is not the case that the designers of family-room kitchens were seeking inspiration from working-class models. Instead one could look to clients' changing manners. In the later nineteenth century, middle-class householders wanted to make clear distinctions between their own housing and that of working-class households in order to mark their superior status. One way to do this was to insist on correct manners, which required the separation of cooking from dining, and to locate reception rooms at the front, work rooms at the rear of houses. The relaxation of this anxiety in post-World War II life, and more informal manners in general, allowed middle-class householders to welcome the relaxed sociability of great-room kitchens, probably oblivious to the fact that they were replicating some aspects of working-class triple-decker or tenement socializing.

Dining rooms as separate spaces for sociability and entertaining developed to their maturity in the eighteenth century. Although they still used parlors or chambers, householders and guests preferred to gather in commodious dining rooms with finely carved ornament or expensive, painted decoration. They enjoyed food and drink in dining rooms, but also used that room as an informal parlor for conversation. By the later eighteenth century, dining rooms had usurped parlors as the largest room for receiving guests. Dining rooms through the nineteenth century also had elaborate architectural decoration. Suites of dining-room furniture manufactured to produce a harmonious appearance unified the dining room's décor while providing ample support for numerous guests to dine and converse.

While setting aside a separate room for dining in the nineteenth century became common for mid-budget households, at the working-class pole families ate in general-purpose living rooms or in kitchens that had enough room for a table. Informal habits in the late twentieth century led many to eating meals in open-plan kitchen-dining-family rooms where tables supplemented by a counter with stools provided additional eating space. As formally structured meals became less common, householders could take their plates to disparate parts of the house. Even bathrooms sometimes shelter a couple's private meals.

4

SLEEPING, HEALTH, AND PRIVACY

Houses for modern people always come with spaces designed to protect the health of bodies—either through giving them dedicated places to sleep or through appliances and systems designed to support privacy, cleanliness, and a healthful environment. Seventeenth-century householders had neither bedrooms nor bathrooms but instead chose some places in the house to temporarily lay down a bed, perhaps in the form of a sack of feathers, and used the outdoors to dispose of human wastes.

In bedrooms people have concretized notions about the proper relations of family members to each other, and the proper relation of the sleeping axis—what I term the constellation of all the sleeping spaces—to the rest of domestic space and daily life. Tracing this movement from the seventeenth into the nineteenth century, we see that sleeping in a bedroom in the seventeenth century was a historical achievement, yet by the nineteenth century it was common practice.

The general development of bedrooms through the first half of the twentieth century led to purifying the room of extraneous activities and focusing ever more on the bed and activities proper to it. Dinners were moved to dining rooms; storage to cellars, attics, and closets; washing to bathrooms. Nonetheless in addition to sleeping, bedrooms at times served to display the newborn members of the family and to bid farewell to the deceased ones. In recent decades bedrooms for teenagers or elderly family members have often become studio-apartment-like enclaves with chairs, desks, couches, and computers, and modern sleepers have added watching television in bed.

Washing the body was rarely done in the seventeenth and eighteenth centuries, so a special space for this activity was not included in houses. Indoor wastes were deposited in chamber pots, kept under beds or in a commode in other rooms, and emptied outdoors by householders or servants.[1] Bodily wastes were disposed of outdoors in outhouses or privies, or just in a ditch. Radical was the idea of setting aside specific rooms in a house for the purposes of managing bodily wastes and maintaining cleanliness. That required a late nineteenth-century rethinking of equipment from casual to permanent and from outdoors to in. In the bedroom and bathroom, Americans have negotiated and expressed historically changing concepts of what is healthy, what is clean, what is polite, what is public, and what is private.

Bedding Down in Seventeenth- and Eighteenth-Century Houses

Many seventeenth-century houses had only one room, and sleeping occurred wherever there was space. Travelers who asked for shelter at such a house might find themselves sleeping in a shed on a pile of deer skins, not on a bed. Ranged around the inside of half of a Texas governor's 1690 one-room house were ten beds constructed of a "rug made of reeds," each held upon four forked sticks.[2] We imagine these beds as a cross between a basket and a hammock. In the other half of the house there were some shelves holding storage baskets used for foodstuffs. Stowing foodstuffs on shelves was akin and adjacent to stowing visitors in their bunks—early arrangements for sleeping afforded no privacy and often required sharing a sleeping room or a bed with strangers.

Like the Texas governor's house, East-Coast Anglo houses of one room incorporated beds and sleeping in the same room with cooking, eating, and socializing, sometimes providing extra sleeping space in an attic. The Whipple House in Ipswich, Massachusetts, was begun c. 1655 as a single-room plan with a sleeping chamber in the attic (some New England single-room houses still exist, but only as the core of a house that was later expanded). A similar one-room house called Pear Valley with a sleeping attic, built about 1740, still stands on the Eastern Shore of Maryland.[3] Since one-room houses must incorporate all the indoor activities into a single space, dwellers invented movable furniture, such as tip-up beds, which would stand up against the wall and clear room for the next activity after sleeping was finished.

As first-generation settlers prospered in America, they expanded those one-room houses. A hall and a parlor constituted a typical two-room house in the Massachusetts Bay era. The hall was an all-purpose room incorporating portable mattresses made of cloth cases and filled with leaves, cornhusks, or feathers, which were laid on the hall floor at night. The parlor was the special room of the hall-parlor pair reserved for higher-ranking people

Fig. 42. To maximize floor space in the one- and two-room houses of the seventeenth and eighteenth centuries, people relied on movable beds (the mattresses) and bedsteads, storing them in daytime. This is a tip-up bedstead, hinged to store upright against the wall. Other storable beds of the era took the form of cloth sacks filled with dry leaves, corn husks, or feathers. Photo E. C. Cromley.

Fig. 43. This fine eighteenth-century bedstead belonged to Philadelphia botanist John Bartram. In the seventeenth century, the owners' bedstead could typically be found in the parlor or chamber, along with storage furniture and a table and chairs used to entertain guests. A mix of private activity and hospitality characterized early parlors or chambers—a mix that was to be sorted into separate rooms for sleeping in larger houses of the eighteenth century. Photo E. C. Cromley.

and activities; owners would keep their bedstead in the parlor (see fig. 2, Boardman House hall-parlor plan, in chapter 1). Beside the bed a dining table and chairs enabled the householders to entertain small groups for dinner. The owners' beautifully furnished bedstead provided a showpiece to impress dinner guests, while storage chests in the parlor held plates, table and bed linens, clothing, eating utensils, and drinking vessels.

Hall-parlor houses often expanded onto a second floor, which provided extra sleeping space for children and servants. A ladder gave simple access to the upper level, but boxed stairs were common in more developed two-room houses. Householders with more resources added a third room, a cooking kitchen. An extra sleeping room could be built adjacent to or above the new kitchen, where it benefited from the cooking fireplace's heat. If the main cooking fireplace was removed to the addition, it opened up the possibility for the old hall to become a more informal service and sleeping room that supported light household work and beds instead of cooking.

Some people remained in one-room houses through the eighteenth century, and some retained earlier attitudes and slept wherever there was a place to lie down, while the elite began to build separated private chambers for their beds. The elaborate bedsteads and specialized bed textiles called "bed furniture," previously found in a parlor, would be moved to a separate chamber. For even more firmly separating a private zone, builders created the chamber floor on a second level. The idea of a separate floor for bedrooms persists today.

In eighteenth-century Virginia, dedicated bedrooms were found in the great houses of plantation families and also in outbuildings nearby. Philip Fithian recorded in his 1770s diary the sleeping rooms in the Carter family's house. Upstairs "one room is for Mr. & Mrs. Carter; the second for the young ladies; & the other two for occasional company."[4] The upper bedrooms in the house were not sufficient to sleep all the household members, however. Behind the main house was a school-room block, forty-five by twenty-seven feet, with three main-floor rooms and two rooms on the second floor. Philip Fithian and two of the Carter sons used these second-floor rooms as their bedrooms. When Fithian visited Col. Tayloe's house, he observed that near the great house were two two-story stone houses. One was a kitchen and the other was used for a nursery and sleeping rooms.[5]

The changing types of furniture found in an eighteenth-century bedchamber show how this room was gradually purged of extraneous uses

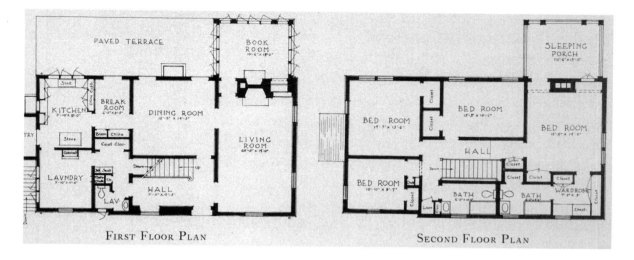

FIRST FLOOR PLAN   SECOND FLOOR PLAN

Fig. 44. By the later eighteenth century, the idea of a "chamber floor" gained popularity. Well-to-do householders enhanced privacy by locating family bedrooms or chambers on an upper floor, apart from both reception rooms on the entrance floor and service spaces like the kitchen. By the 1920s it was the norm for householders at upper- and middle-income levels to secure privacy for sleeping and bathing by locating these rooms on a separate floor in houses with more than one floor. This house also has a sleeping porch. James Cleaves house in Winchester, Massachusetts, by architects Eleanor Raymond and Henry Frost; in E. Power, *The Smaller American House* (1927).

such as dinner parties to focus on beds and sleeping. Lists of furnishings found in the probate inventories produced after the owner's death often record the household's furnishings grouped by the room they were in. Using such inventories, historian Kevin Sweeney studied how bed chambers developed in Wethersfield, Connecticut over eight decades. At the beginning of his study in 1721, a ground-floor room called "best chamber" began to replace the parlor as the site for the best bed. Sets of chairs and a table were still found in the best chamber, which indicates that entertaining visitors remained an important function of the bedchamber.[6] Between 1721 and 1760 the typical amount of furniture in a Wethersfield household more than doubled and the average household had about three bedsteads. For nearly half of the households, the best bed still stood in the parlor, but at least 40 percent of all beds were found in second story chambers or garrets. But by the end of the eighteenth century the best bed was most likely to be in a room given over to sleeping only, whether that room was on the ground floor or the second. The parents' sleeping apartment became, Sweeney says, a room used almost exclusively for sleeping according to the furniture listed in the inventory.[7]

Rooms in inventories might be called "bedrooms," but their usage included mixed storage in houses that were too small to afford a purified room for sleeping.[8] A small two-story Delaware house inhabited by a poor family had one undifferentiated space upstairs. As seen in their household inventory, they stored a bed, three old chairs, several spinning wheels, seven sickles, and half a barrel of tar in the upstairs bedroom.

Modest Nineteenth-Century Sleeping Spaces

Americans who had settled cities and towns along the East Coast in the eighteenth and early nineteenth century did not all prosper. Looking for more fertile farmland, for work opportunities, or simply for adventure, they began to move into unsettled areas, encouraged by federal programs that granted them land and required them to build a house. Log houses, earthen structures, and even underground shelters housed them at first with few of the conveniences that some settlers were accustomed to.

In accounts of sleeping in newly built or older rustic houses, travelers and settlers describe a significant lack of sleeping comfort compared to cities and settled areas. Richard Cordley was a missionary from Andover (Massachusetts) Theological Seminary sent to Christianize Kansas in 1857. On the road, he and his driver spent the night in an Indian cabin. "My bed was a shelf on the side of the cabin supported by pins driven into the logs. There were several such shelves around the walls . . . my shelf looked neater and cleaner than the others and was evidently the spare bed of the house. It was about a foot and a half from the floor, and had some sort of blanket on it."[9] "All round the cabin the family lay on their shelves."[10] The cabin was fifteen by fifteen feet, of log construction, but with no chinking; he could look out into the yard between the logs.

As travelers, Cordley and church friends stopped at another Native American village and spent the night. After supper they were invited "into the large unfinished half-story chamber of the cabin. Here the kind people had prepared for our comfort by spreading around on the floor blankets and quilts and buffalo robes, and the many substitutes for beds known only to the elastic hospitality of the frontier. But to our weary bodies an Indian blanket and a cotton-wood board were as good as a bed of down."[11]

Sleeping arrangements were minimal when Cordley arrived in Lawrence, Kansas, his first parish. The town was smaller than expected and crammed with travelers—all available rooms were taken. "An officer of the church kindly took me in. . . . He was living in the kitchen of his unfinished house. A cot in the open garret served me for a bed, and some sort of a stand in the unfinished parlor, where the carpenters were at work, had to serve me for a study table." He lived there for three weeks.[12] "Every tenement and shanty, every sod cabin and tent, fairly swarmed with occupants. There would be two or three families in a house, and each family keeping board-

SALT LAKE CITY IN 1850.

Fig. 45. A period drawing of one-room frontier houses in a sketch of Salt Lake City in 1850. These small houses represent the kind of house described in travelers' western diaries. Mattresses filled with feathers, leaves, corn husks, or other comfort-aiding materials were laid on any unoccupied section of the floor (or in a bed frame or bedstead). Samuel Manning, "Salt Lake City in 1850," in *American Pictures Drawn with Pen and Pencil* (London: Religious Tract Society, 1876), 69. Courtesy of Winterthur Library, Printed Book and Periodical Collection.

ers."[13] The privacy observed in households in settled cities and towns was not available.

Pioneering where she was born in 1878 in the town of Florence, Arizona, Edith Stratton Kitt recorded her memories of sleeping arrangements. In their house on a ranch, the walls were made of cedar posts, standing vertically like fence posts, and the spaces between the posts were filled in with mud chinking. The large front room had a bed on either side of the front door, and the parents' bed was made of lumber, while the children's bed was of mesquite poles laced with rawhide in place of bed springs. Edith's mother used to tie her to the bedpost for safety from rattlesnakes.[14]

The family later moved to Tucson, Arizona. Ms Kitt reported that in the 1880s people built small, one-story houses right to the street edge.[15] In the extreme heat of the summer, people moved their beds outdoors. "In summer some of the people who had no patios pulled their cots out onto the sidewalks and went to bed" so you had to walk down the middle of the street.[16] Thus privacy in sleeping was easily given up for a bed in cooler air.

African American scholar W. E. B. Du Bois wrote about his experience with bedrooms when he was a teacher in Tennessee in the 1880s. He boarded with the families of students at his school, including at Doc Burke's farm. "They lived in a one-and-a-half-room cabin in the hollow of the farm . . . the front room was full of great fat white beds, scrupulously neat . . . at first I used to be a little alarmed at the approach of bedtime in the one lone bedroom, but embarrassment was very deftly avoided. First, all the children nodded and slept, and were stowed away in one great pile of goose feathers; next, the mother and the father discreetly slipped away to the kitchen while

I went to bed; then, blowing out the dim light, they retired in the dark. In the morning all were up and away before I thought of awakening."[17] The family made up for lack of privacy built into the architecture with privacy created by manners and the timing of sleep-related activities.

In the 1890s Du Bois went to live in Dougherty County, Georgia. He observed that some of the African Americans there lived in the same cabins they had lived in in slavery days, while others lived in cabins built more recently. About fifteen hundred African American families lived outside of Albany, Georgia in 1898. Most families lived in one- and two-room houses, which had to accommodate all the household inhabitants and activities without the privacy that several rooms might allow. Du Bois wrote, "All over the face of the land is the one room cabin . . . it is nearly always old and bare, built of rough boards, and neither plastered nor ceiled. Light and ventilation are supplied by the single door and by the square hole in the wall with its wooden shutter. There is no glass, porch, or ornamentation without. Within is a fireplace, black and smoky, and usually unsteady with age. A bed or two, a table, a wooden chest, and a few chairs compose the furniture."[18]

Although we tend to think of crowding as being characteristic of homes for the poor in cities, Du Bois wrote, in rural Georgia all the cabins were crowded, too. In Dougherty County, Georgia, he found large families of eight and ten occupying one or two rooms, and "for every 10 rooms of house accommodations, for the blacks there are 25 persons, which is worse accommodations than in New York City tenements. . . . The single great ad-

Fig. 46. Wyollah slave cottage in Adams County, Mississippi. W. E. B. DuBois observed that in the later nineteenth century most rural African Americans lived in cabins the same as the ones they had lived in under slavery. He described boarding with a family, c. 1880, where the adults and the children all slept in one room of the two-room house. Photo E. C. Cromley.

vantage of the Negro peasant is that he may spend most of his life outside his hovel, in the open fields." Did he mean that people also slept outdoors to escape interior crowding?[19]

In nineteenth-century cities, investors and developers built tenements—multi-family buildings for three or more households—providing rental units for poor people. How did working-class city-dwellers sleep? In New York City the reformer Alfred Tredway White built workers' housing in 1890. His Riverside Buildings were six-story blocks of apartments. The typical apartment had rooms called living room, parlor, and bedroom. Although the "parlor" label on the plan for White's Riverside Apartments suggests more sociable uses of space, we know from photographic and other evidence that tenement dwellers slept in all the rooms of their apartments.

In working-class tenement units the numbers of people who needed beds depended on the size of the family and on whether there were boarders who supplemented the family income. Tenants often took in boarders to help them meet their expenses, and boarders needed additional beds. When there was a large number of sleepers, not just bedrooms but also the parlor and living room/kitchen were enlisted as sleeping space, and individual beds were shared. Kitchens were sometimes preferred over bedrooms for sleeping because they were the warmest rooms.

The New York tenement family's cleanliness depended on a well and pump in the yard and a privy behind the building, but no bathtub. Critics charged that providing bathtubs was pointless because laborers would only use the tub to store coal and preferred not to wash themselves. Resisting this norm, A. T. White installed basement bathtubs for residents' use. He believed that tenement dwellers wanted to keep clean just as the middle class did. Early twentieth-century changes in tenement law required that each household have its own bathtub, typically retrofitted into the kitchen; some cities also provided public bath buildings to make up for the lack of private bathtubs in the early twentieth century.[20]

Early tenement buildings often had privies in the backyard rather than indoor toilets. Starting in New York in 1879, new laws required that indoor bathrooms with flush toilets be provided for every two tenement households. When the city of New York held hearings in preparation for a new 1901 tenement law, dwellers testified that they had to move out of their older tenement building when the ill-maintained privy overflowed.

Enslaved African Americans lived in houses and slept in spaces not their own—cabins and shacks in agricultural landscapes, residual spaces in

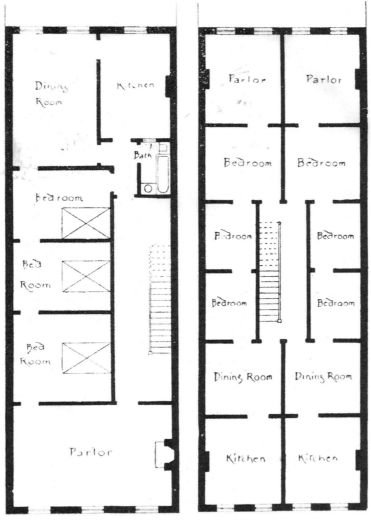

Fig. 2. New York Tenement-house before 1879.

Fig. 3. Double Tenement-house in New York before 1879.

Fig. 47. Tenement apartment plans for two units per floor as built in New York before 1879. Census records and dwellers' testimony show that all rooms were used to sleep the dense populations of tenement districts. Windowless bedrooms were outlawed by a New York 1879 law. *American Architect and Building News* 29 (Sept. 27, 1890): 195.

plantation houses and outbuildings, or leftover spaces provided by their urban enslavers.[21] Housing for enslaved people on southern plantations was sometimes self-built, sometimes constructed by plantation owners to frame and enhance the appearance of the main house. Slave quarters were built near the enslaver's house, or enslaved household workers lived in the main house, sleeping in family bedrooms. Attics and loft spaces provided enough room to lay down on a simple mattress. A recreation of a dormitory for enslaved women is now part of George Washington's Mt. Vernon, one of the numerous small buildings that cluster around Washington's main house. Frederick Douglass, later a famous orator, recounts his spatial

Fig. 48. Houses for the enslaved workers on plantations were sometimes self-built, sometimes built to match the style of other outbuildings on a large estate. This replica slave house reproduced at George Washington's Mt. Vernon in Virginia demonstrates multiple beds in a dormitory for enslaved women. Photo E. C. Cromley.

Fig. 49. Servants in prosperous households often lived in attics with cast-off furniture. Advice columns in late nineteenth and early twentieth-century magazines urged employers to give their servants healthy and attractive rooms. This small servant's room at Biltmore (Asheville, NC) from the early twentieth century was provided with a metal bed frame, known to repel bedbugs and be easy to keep clean. Photo E. C. Cromley.

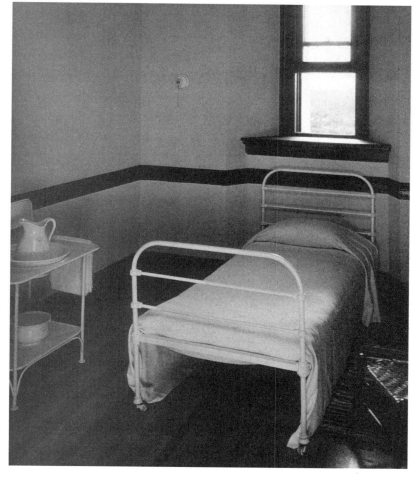

experience trying to find some privacy to learn to read in his sleeping loft in the house of his Maryland enslaver. Enslaved individuals were forbidden to read, so he had to conceal his desire. He slept in a loft above the kitchen, so he "crammed a flour barrel and a chair" up the ladder into his loft space to serve him as a study.[22]

Well-to-do households were populated by indentured servants, enslaved workers, apprentices, and hired help who, along with the householders themselves, executed the work of feeding the residents, laundering linens and clothing, and cleaning up. By the mid-nineteenth century, middle-class householders had begun to pay more attention to servants' comfort and to recognize their need for rooms of their own.

In her 1840 book *The House Book*, Eliza Leslie suggested the following furnishings for servants' rooms: painted, low-post bedsteads; unbleached linen sheets for summer and unbleached cotton sheets for winter; one comfortable-type quilt per bed, which she described as just as warm as three blankets; a piece of carpet by the side of each bed in winter; and in each room a washing table, a looking glass, a table, and several chairs. If there were no closets, a few shelves and some pegs or hooks for hanging clothes should be put up.[23] Starting at mid-century servants' rooms appear on house plans as specially designed spaces, small but ventilated, sometimes with closets for possessions, and sometimes with a bath. Household advice-book authors take up the cause of making servants more comfortable with ideas about furnishing the servant's room and ornamenting it with color or art, rugs, and curtains. They recommended providing washing materials, but no bathtubs, for clean bodies.

Nineteenth-Century Toileting and Bathing Spaces

Middle-class standards for bodily cleanliness were slow to develop. By the mid-nineteenth century portable bathtubs were in widespread use if a household had a servant to fill and empty the tub. Baths could be taken in a kitchen near the stove that produced a hot water supply or in bedrooms where servants delivered hot water. Taking baths in front of a heat source such as a bedroom fireplace was preferred. Bedrooms often had a little stand with a pitcher of water and a basin, which people would use to wash parts of the body in the era before plumbed bathrooms. Indeed this equipment lived on after bathrooms became common.

A commode was a piece of furniture made to hold a chamber pot,

Fig. 50. *Opposite*, A mother tucks her child into bed with portable bathtub on the floor below, 1889. Portable bathtubs allowed nineteenth-century inhabitants to take baths once in a while. Servants did the hard work of filling and emptying the tub. It was often set up in front of a fireplace to take the chill off. Emma C. Hewitt, *Queen of the Home* (Oakland, CA: H. J. Smith, 1889), 220.

Fig. 51a. *Opposite, left*, A pitcher and basin were kept in bedrooms before plumbed bathrooms could be relied upon for washing the body. Small sinks installed in bedrooms sometimes replaced the pitcher and basin, but householders afraid of sewer gas eschewed any bedroom plumbing. Photo E. C. Cromley.

Fig. 51b. *Opposite, right*, A patent "combination bathtub" with bathing in either tub or shower, sitting or standing; advertised by the Wheeling Sanitary Manufacturing Co. in *American Builder* 37 (1924).

A Combination Bath Tub

— PATENTED —

One size only, for all size people

Regular Bath, Seat Bath, Shower Bath, Foot Bath, and Child's Bath, all in one piece

Made of Semi-Vitreous Porcelain Ware
and
Enameled Iron Ware

Enameled Iron Ware, 44x30 inches to tile in corner only. Painted white front. Waste in foot section either right or left hand end. Only one size made.

Testimonials

Semi-Vitreous Porcelain Ware, 44x30 inches to tile in right or left hand corner, or in rooms. Enameled white all sides. Only one size made.

Mr. T. E. Keller, 150 E. 125th St., New York City, says:
"I had installed in my house several months ago one of your Combination Bath Tubs fitted complete with shower and curtain, and I cannot say too much in recommending this fixture and also when I decided on this new type of tub, as it gives the bathroom features that other patterns tube do not have.

"I am a man weighing two hundred pounds and the tube have ample room for one of my size to properly bathe.

"You are at liberty to use this letter in any way to advance the use of this fixture, as I cheerfully recommend this tub to anyone, and if I were to again another bathroom for my own use, or for sale, I would use this Combination Tub."

Dr. Norman N. Burnham, 1414 Ogden Ave., Chicago, Ill., installed one of these tubs in his new residence a year ago, and remarks as follows:

"It is the best fixture I ever saw, and I would not be without it for anything. It is most economical in the use of hot water, and this is a decided advantage where instantaneous gas water heaters are used. Furthermore, it is an ideal tub where there are children, as it can be used in advantageous as a foot tub; by the children comes in dirty from playing. The shower feature is also an advantage which greatly adds. In fact, this tub is most acceptable in every way, and I most thoroughly recommend this fixture."

Mrs. Burnham is equally as enthusiastic as the Doctor, and states: "It is a wonderful bath."

Sold through jobbers of plumbing supplies. Write us for descriptive circular.

Wheeling Sanitary Mfg. Co.
Wheeling, W. Va.

Vitreous China-Closet, Bowls and Flush Tanks of all kinds
Semi-Vitreous Porcelain, Baths, Kitchen Sinks, Lavatories, Drinking Fountains, Urinal Stalls, etc.
Enameled Iron—Baths on feet and on base.

Branch Office and Show Room   315 Wrigley Building, Chicago, Illinois

Fig. 52. A commode held a chamber pot in the era before flush toilets disposed of human waste; it could be in the form of a chair with a removable chamber pot, or might look like a chest or cabinet that revealed its chamber pot when opened. Advertisement for Universal Commode Cabinet, *Decorator and Furnisher* (February 1884): 184.

providing the user with an indoor alternative to a visit to the privy, with a more comfortable seat and a lid to cover the contents. The new concept of indoor toilets, made possible by the invention of the flush mechanism and the plumbed toilet, became available in the later nineteenth century. However, many householders resisted introducing odors and germs into the clean household and preferred to keep toilet activity outdoors in the traditional privy. By the turn of the twentieth century, fixed bathtubs replaced portable ones, installed in a bathroom dedicated to the purpose. These were plumbed to deliver hot and cold water with a drain to empty the tub when the bath was finished, so servants were no longer needed to fill and empty a tub.

Fig. 53a and Fig. 53b. Outdoors the privy or outhouse, seen here at nineteenth-century workers' housing in Batsto, New Jersey, served the same purpose as a toilet in today's houses. The seats in the Poplar Hill, Maryland, privy are at three different heights to accommodate the different size members of the family. Photos E. C. Cromley.

To make toilet and washing facilities really work, a reliable water supply was needed. By the early years of the nineteenth century, some cities such as Portsmouth, New Hampshire had piped water from companies that had taken the initiative to lay pipelines to subscribers' houses. Iron cookstoves sometimes heated water in tanks that could be pumped to bathtubs, and in large houses a cistern might solve the problem of delivering water. Cisterns on the top floor or roof of a house caught rainwater or were filled by pumping water up from a well; then gravity fed the water down into plumbed fixtures. In the early twentieth century plumbing delivered city-supplied water to indoor sinks, bathtubs, and toilets in increasing numbers of middle- and upper-class houses.

Fig. 54a and Fig. 54b. Modern bathrooms with their standard three fixed and plumbed receptacles— toilet, sink, bathtub—became the norm for the prosperous classes, and by the early twentieth century were adopted by all classes who could afford them. "Model Bathroom for the Average Dwelling," from E. S. Keene, *Mechanics of the Household* (1918), 97. Upper-class households had bathrooms with decorative features. *Country Life in America* 4 (September 1903): 356.

The earlier chamber pot or commode that had provided toilet facilities in several rooms including bedrooms migrated in its new form, the plumbed toilet, to a bathroom near the bedrooms. Likewise the formerly portable tub, often used near warm parts of the house like the kitchen or bedroom fireplace, shifted to the bathroom in the form of a fixed tub. Other locations for washing and toileting—outdoors or in the kitchen—were given up by modernizers in favor of consolidation in a single room.[24] The three-fixture bathroom—tub, toilet, and sink—finally collected all the washing and toileting equipment into one room; typically, one bathroom was shared among all the household. Such bathrooms preserved privacy by having one door opening from a hall or corridor, often on the second floor of houses where bedrooms were located. Rural householders who did not have access to piped water had to wait for these conveniences. Sears Roebuck catalogs sold composting toilets into the 1930s that did not need a water supply, appealing to mothers tired of making midnight trips to the privy with a child.

Nineteenth-Century Middle- and Upper-Middle-Class Sleeping

In towns and cities, as well as wealthier rural areas, the private bedroom spread as a norm from elite to middle-class households. This dedicated bedroom was separated by walls and doors from social and service rooms, and was well established in the early nineteenth century. After c. 1840, popular architectural advice books conveyed house designs with chamber floors to a broad middle- and upper-class readership. Kinds of bedrooms proliferated in advice literature to encompass not just family bedrooms but guest rooms and carefully arranged servants' rooms. Children's rooms got ever more attention. In later nineteenth-century pattern-book designs, most chamber floors also have one bathroom with a bathtub, a sink, and a water closet.

New kinds of space-saving bedroom furniture came on the market in the later nineteenth century to help people furnish small houses and apartments. Stylish furniture in a variety of woods and finishes was mass produced, marketed in suites, and made specific to different domestic uses—kitchen chairs were not the same as bedroom chairs. A parlor bed published in 1884 in the *Decorator and Furnisher* magazine shows the Victorian version of the hinged tip-up bed that seventeenth-century dwellers had found useful. A patent for "A New Extension Bed," published in an 1898 *Scientific American* calls for a bedstead made of metal that could be adjusted in both length and width by sliding rails. "Among the many advantages claimed for this bed are its structural firmness and its ready adjustability to conform with the accommodations afforded by various rooms."[25] This suggests that the size of rooms and not the sizes of people, mattresses, sheets, or blankets controlled dimensions for beds. Another piece of patented furniture was a bed that folded up to look just like a fireplace.[26] Many such combinations were patented in the nineteenth century claiming to make it easier for inhabitants to furnish small dwellings. Built-in beds were popular in the

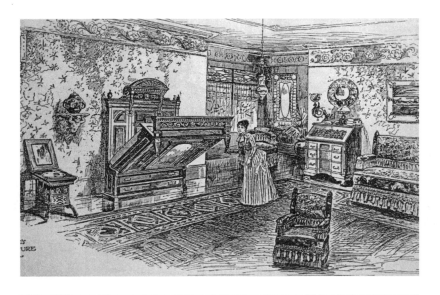

Fig. 55a and Fig. 55b. The US Patent Office preserves numerous patent applications for folding, expanding, collapsing, and multiuse beds from the era of small rental units. A tip-up bed like this one allowed the renters to furnish a small apartment and turn a daytime parlor into a bedroom at night. *Decorator and Furnisher* 17 (1891): 19. Many small houses of the 1920s had hinged "door beds" as used in the White Efficiency Apartment that were hidden in a living-room closet and let down at night.

THE "WHITE" EFFICIENCY APARTMENT IN DETAIL

The illustrations below show glimpses of the "White" Door Bed and Space Saving Devices as they actually appear in the "White" Efficiency Apartment. Each one adds its share to the comfort and convenience of the whole.

"WHITE" DOOR BEDS
and Space Saving Devices

1920s; they occupied closets that, when opened, revealed a bed that turned around and rested on the living-room floor.

Most bedrooms on chamber floors in eighteenth- and nineteenth-century urban and suburban houses had independent doors from separate routes of circulation, so one did not enter a bedroom by walking through an adjacent room but by walking through a hall or corridor. Such circulation arrangements testify to a growing interest in privacy not just from outsiders but also from other family members. Sometimes adjacent bedrooms had a connecting doorway, which facilitated specially negotiated privacy relationships of child and parent, or caregiver and invalid, or in some instances, husband and wife.

In the Hispanic tradition, as seen in New Mexico, traditional houses were typically built as a long string of rooms wrapped around an inner courtyard. The Watrous House, built in 1849, demonstrates the courtyard plan. The covered porch that runs around part of the courtyard serves the purpose of a corridor, and instead of halls, rooms have doors opening to other rooms. Bedrooms may be entered from adjacent rooms as well as from the outdoors, as if each room was a sort of separate house. Bedrooms thus become more public than they would have been in houses with more passages or corridors that controlled the zoning of interior privacy.

Hispanic tradition encouraged a broad entrance hall, or zaguan, as a centerpiece. In houses in New Mexico this center hall was easily adapted in the twentieth century for uses besides circulation. Householders eager to modernize their houses thought the end of the center hall seemed an appropriate size and location to wall off for an indoor bathroom, for example.[27] Meanwhile, others felt that the generous size of the center hall made it a good location for the children's beds.

Woodward's 1869 *National Architect* can serve as a useful compendium of bedroom and bathroom ideas aimed at all income levels. In his Design No. 13, all six bedrooms are relegated to the chamber floor, where there is also a bathing room for a tub. These rooms differ in size and quality from each other; while the largest bedroom has a fireplace, windows on two sides, and two sizeable closets, the three smaller bedrooms provide smaller closets, and two of the remaining bedrooms have no closet. None of the bedrooms are accessed by means of an adjacent room, but all open into a hall. There is, however, a communicating door from one bedroom into the adjacent one "so that in case of necessity they could be used in connection."[28] Such an arrangement helped mothers have quick access to small

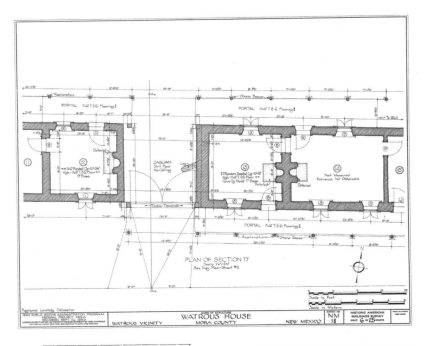

Fig. 56a and Fig. 56b. The Watrous House, Mora County, New Mexico, built in 1849, demonstrates the Hispanic courtyard plan. In houses of this sort bedrooms may be entered from adjacent rooms as well as from the outdoors, as if each room is a sort of separate house. No separate indoor circulation system of halls or corridors moves people through the house. Plans from the Historic American Buildings Survey.

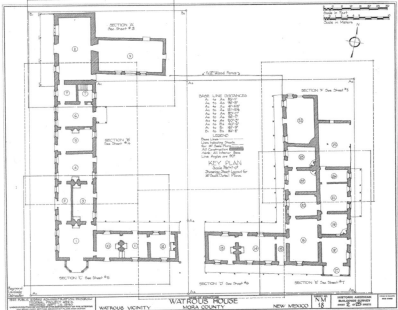

children. This chamber floor provides variations in size, storage, heat, and light for family members with differing levels of importance and different claims on spaciousness or convenience.

Urban houses for prosperous families in the latter half of the nineteenth century were particularly well arranged for zoning the bedroom areas of

Fig. 57. Louisiana plantation houses sometimes included garçonnières, or special freestanding buildings of bedrooms, for the single males of the household and their guests. Householders isolated the disruptive energy and noise of the guys in these units at Destrehan Plantation. Photo E. C. Cromley.

the house. The first floor or two of an urban row house in the 1870s and 1880s typically contained an entrance hall, front and back parlors, and often a dining room. On the floors above the reception rooms were chambers for the various family members, and on the attic floor were often found servants' bedrooms. In a four- or five-story house, the separate functions of the house were very clearly demarcated on different floors.

In the great plantation houses of Louisiana one can find chamber floors where bedrooms are assured their privacy, but in addition there are features called garçonnières. These garçonnières, first used in the nineteenth century, were separate, freestanding buildings linked to the main plantation house, constructed for the young men in the family where they would have bedrooms and rooms for socializing. The plantation called Destrehan offers an example of this—its main house was built in 1787 and rebuilt in the 1840s in a Greek revival style. Two-story verandas on three sides surround the main body of the house, and butting up against the verandas are two two-story garçonnières. These kept the older boys' activity a little segregated from the main family in their dwelling, where noisy parties or questionable behaviors would not impinge on adult peace and quiet. At another

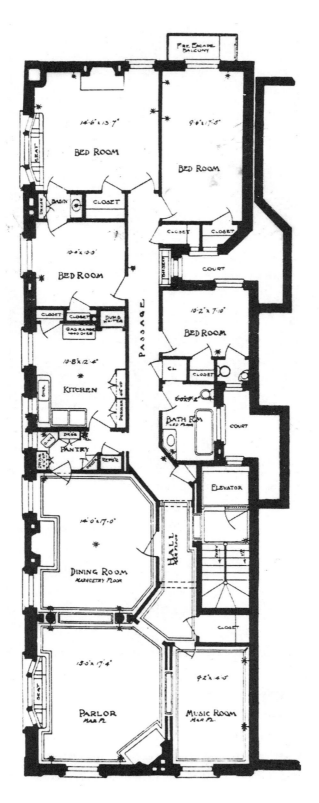

Fig. 58. Plan of a one-floor apartment at 78 Irving Place. Architects solved the arrangement of bedrooms in a one-floor unit when the budget and the building envelope afforded them enough latitude. Grouping reception rooms near the front door and utility rooms—kitchen, bathroom—near the best ventilation allowed chambers or bedrooms to have their own grouping where they could be kept private from visitors' view. *Architectural Record* 11 (July 1901): 495.

plantation, Houmas House, the 1840s garçonnières stand somewhat farther from the main house. The garçonnières, without plumbing, would have provided only shelter and privacy but not all the conveniences for the older sons of the family and visiting men.[29]

For those who needed to economize by building single-story houses, bedroom location had to be thought through differently than in multi-storied houses. In his 1889 book *Convenient Houses*, Louis Gibson supplied a chapter on one-floor houses.[30] Economical designs such as Louis Gibson's located bedrooms contiguous to the more social rooms, creating problems for those who treasured privacy. Plan No. 19 has two chambers, a kitchen, a sitting room, and a parlor. The chamber at the front opens into the parlor, into the sitting room through a pocket door, and into the hall. The second chamber opens only into the hall. Such a one-floor house can give flexibility in room uses, and often Gibson labeled rooms with use options—for example, "bedroom or sitting room"—indicating latitude in how the space should be used. But used as a bedroom, the room's contiguity to parlor or dining could disrupt ideals of privacy.

Following an older custom of locating important people in a ground-floor chamber, some nineteenth-century households in multi-storied houses still provided rooms for parents, visitors, the sick, or the elderly in ground-floor bedrooms. Author William Dean Howells visited Mark Twain in Hartford and was invited to use an elaborately decorated ground-floor bedroom with its own bath in an almost separate wing of the house. It was divided from the drawing room by a hallway and was near the quiet library. Carl Gustavus Adolphus Voight of Grand Rapids, Michigan built a house in 1895 where he and his wife occupied the ground floor. Their chamber housed its 1860s bedstead from their early married years, out of step with the 1890s decor of the rest of the house. Their bedroom was near the kitchen and served as a sickroom later, "another common Victorian use for lower-floor bedrooms."[31]

In the years before the funeral industry had established itself, family deaths were managed at home and the bodies of the deceased laid out in parlors or bedrooms. Friends and family members who wanted to pay respects to the departed would come to view the body at rest in his or her bedroom, which became, for the occasion, a public space. Likewise, bedrooms became reception rooms when visitors came to see a new mother and her baby.

Fig. 59. Health advice, from the mid-nineteenth through the early twentieth century, focused on making bedrooms dust-free, bug-free, and well ventilated. Bedroom curtains, pillows, bedspreads, wallpaper, and carpets were all criticized as dust-catchers. An iron bedstead, shown in Gervase Wheeler's pattern book, *Rural Homes*, of 1852, was the healthiest since it did not host bedbugs. In spite of bedbugs, people often preferred the ornamental presence of a familiar wooden bed, displayed in a c. 1890 bedroom at the A. J. Miller House, Augusta County, Virginia. Photo E. C. Cromley.

Physical and Mental Health in Bedrooms

Beginning in the mid-nineteenth century numerous health concerns collected around bedrooms, and articles in contemporary magazines gave advice on how to protect a family's health. Parents who tried to make a healthy sleeping environment for their infants were alerted to hidden dangers. If a baby were put to sleep in the same bed with the mother, she might roll over and crush the infant; separate cribs should be provided for each baby.

The dust and dirt generated by industrial cities seemed especially evident in bedrooms, which was especially dangerous, critics said, to innocent sleepers. Every carpet and curtain captured dust that could later threaten the health of a bedroom's occupants. The bedroom furniture itself provided an unwitting home to vermin: bedbugs loved to live in the cracks of beautiful bedsteads.

Finally, health experts raised sex practices and pregnancy as an arena in which bedrooms played a part. Pregnant wives were cautioned not to sleep with their husbands, which experts claimed would risk damage to the de-

Fig. 60a and Fig. 60b. Patent devices to bring fresh air to sleepers included beds that extended partway out the bedroom window, or a tube and a mask that brought the fresh air in to the sleeper. A sleeping porch allowed family members to enhance their exposure to fresh air while sleeping outdoors, as in the James Cleaves house, fig. 44. Many middle-class householders added sleeping porches to their existing bedrooms. "Sleeper in his Indoor Bed Tent," *Scientific American* (Dec. 1909): 416; and "Sleeping Outdoors in the House—Porte-Aire," *Ladies Home Journal* 25 (Sept. 1908): 27.

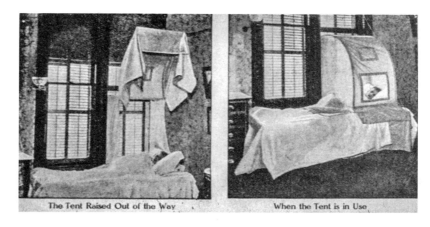

The Tent Raised Out of the Way   When the Tent is in Use

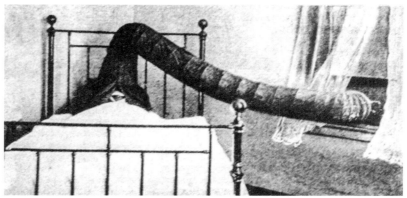

veloping fetus. Husbands had better sleep in their own beds apart from the wife, although perhaps nearby.

An illustration of the bedroom in a New York residence, from Henry Hudson Holly of 1886, indicates the complete set of furnishings that might be found in the bedroom of this era. In addition to the bed with a low foot-board there is also chaise longue and a wicker chair, a desk, a dressing table, a little tea table, an additional chair, and several paintings and ornaments. In Gervase Wheeler's 1852 pattern book, *Rural Homes,* he illustrated bed choices: an iron bed, and a Gothic bed made of carved wood. The carved wooden bed, although beautiful, was believed to hide bedbugs in the joints of the wood. The iron bed, too minimal to be in fashion, nonetheless represented the healthful alternative. Home economist Christine Herrick observed that bugs may lodge in the crevices of wooden bedframes and must be routed with deadly poisons; metal bedsteads, although less handsome, did not harbor insects.[32] The problem was that many people preferred to be fashionable rather than healthy, and iron beds were also associated with

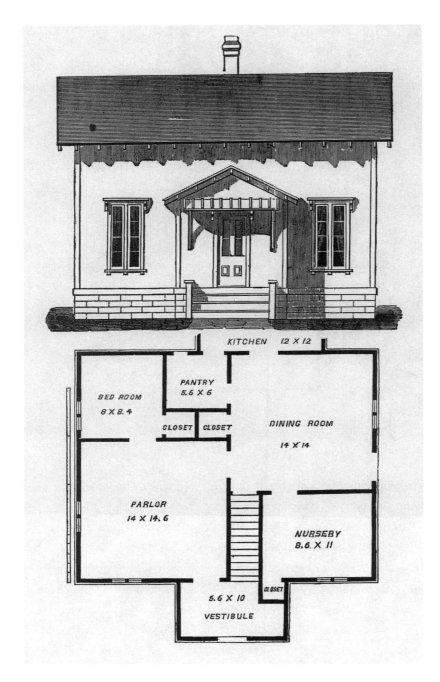

Fig. 61. Writing about home planning, women urged builders to consider the need for a nursery conveniently located near the kitchen. Women who spent many of their housework hours on cooking and child care needed kitchen and nursery to be adjacent. This house plan with a nursery is from 1854. When children reached the age of six or so, they were no longer viewed as children in the general sense, but seen as boys or girls deserving of bedrooms of their own. Oliver Smith, design for a farmhouse, PL 37, *Domestic Architect* (Buffalo: Phinney, 1854).

utilitarian functions and were more commonly found furnishing servants' rooms or sick rooms.[33]

The modern decorator of a bedroom in 1911 should still be especially concerned with fresh air, reported *Good Housekeeping*. As a counter to tuberculosis, doctors recommended sleeping in the fresh air year round. Sleeping porches provided healthful outdoor bedrooms for the wealthy as well as the middle-class sleeper. In California the Greene brothers designed the 1908 Gamble House with three sleeping porches as additions to second-floor bedrooms, integrated into the design of the house. Homeowners added such porches to existing houses. For those without complete outdoor sleeping porches, devices that would allow partial outdoor sleeping could be added to bedroom windows.

The first form of child-specific bedroom in published house plans of the mid-nineteenth century was the nursery. In her 1841 *Treatise on Domestic Economy*, Catherine Beecher encouraged mothers to plan a house in which a nursery room was adjacent to the kitchen. Keeping the child always in sight met the new theories of childrearing in which the mother molded the child's character and trained it in punctuality, honesty, and discipline, qualities needed in the new nineteenth-century economy. Farmhouse nurseries were commonly located in a cluster of ground-floor family rooms as Sally McMurry shows in *Families and Farmhouses in Nineteenth-Century America*. The young children's spaces were linked to the kitchen, sitting room, or dining room. Lucy Ellis planned a farmhouse in 1847 and asserted that having a nursery adjacent to the kitchen and dining room was very important so the mother could "attend to her duties in these several departments."[34] Oliver Smith's 1854 pattern book, *The Domestic Architect*, gives several designs for nurseries that are linked to the sitting room, the dining room, or the family room, and sequestered from the traffic of the entrance hall.

In contrast, urban houses often had nurseries on the second floor where servants, perhaps, tended the children; Calvert Vaux's 1857 *Villas and Cottages* shows nurseries on the chamber floors. Catherine Beecher lamented the fact that many urban houses caused the mother needless stair-climbing effort with the nursery on the second floor and the kitchen in the basement.[35] Children should have for a nursery one of the sunniest and airiest rooms in the house, according to Harriet Beecher Stowe, writing in 1865.[36] The children's chamber should have better sun and a finer view than a guest room used only by transients. While some designs for urban houses and villas had separated the nursery from the kitchen years earlier, historian Sally McMurry notes that in farmhouse design, establishing the nursery distinct from the kitchen was common by c. 1870, giving children a separate space of their own.

The furniture available for a nursery included a crib instead of a cradle. By c. 1850 the crib was de rigueur according to *Godey's Lady's Book*. Since the nursery was not a public room, not intended to receive visitors, cribs of painted metal, functional and cheap, were adequate. Cribs were originally made to sit at the mother's bedside and to be same height as the mother so she could tend or nurse the baby, and they were big enough to contain an infant or a child up to four years old.[37] Reinforced by the American Centennial in 1876, a cradle had become a symbol of America's purer past, clung to as an image long after it had been discarded as useful in the nursery.

In the mid-nineteenth century, children were considered generically—not as individual boys and girls. They were bundled together in shared rooms and not really allowed to express themselves, rather to be seen and not heard. For 1878 authors Williams and Jones, suitable decoration for young children's bedsteads would be the flying cherub, flowers, and birds, since children were assumed to be neither markedly boys nor girls, up to about age six.[38] Older children before the Civil War could not expect a special bedroom in a farmhouse, although new suburban and urban houses were being planned with boys' and girls' bedrooms.[39] Individual bedrooms for older children appear in mid-nineteenth century design books such as Calvert Vaux's. Children were sometimes housed in the small rooms known as "hall bedrooms."[40]

As individuality and self-expression replaced family-group presentation as the goal of the early twentieth century house, bedrooms came to be defined as individual spaces. New bedroom housekeeping principles for young homemakers were articulated by Christine Herrick in 1911; the new practice was to think of each bed as sleeping just one person. Both comfort and health will be improved, she wrote, if two people are put into two single beds rather than one double.[41] Ann Wentworth described to a *House Beautiful* audience how she fixed up sleeping accommodations for seven people in her new house. Each had his or her own room and selected his or her own bedstead and appointments.[42] Even relatively modest households tried to provide a room for each child, or, failing that, separate rooms for the male and female children.

By the 1910s children as individuals got more attention, and clear gender assignments were deemed essential to the mental health of children over the age of six or so. Bedroom decor asserted "masculinity" or "femininity" by the types of fabrics and furnishings deemed appropriate to each gender. For girls, ruffles and dolls, sweetly painted furniture, and a dressing table for primping; for boys, Native American objects or cowboy decorations, chunky wooden furniture, and a workshop space in which to pursue hobbies.[43] Girls' furnishings should help them grow into good wives and mothers, while boys' rooms had storage cabinets to encourage systematic thinking, leading them to become good white-collar workers.

Commercial developers such as the Levitts in the eastern states of New York, New Jersey, and Pennsylvania always included at least two bedrooms, even in very small "starter" houses. Owners of these houses were assisted in expanding them when families grew and more children required additional bedrooms. The builders provided designs for dormers to expand the attic into a chamber floor.[44] After World War II thousands of suburban houses constructed for burgeoning families (the baby boom) aimed to provide individual bedrooms for boys and girls. Twentieth-century teenagers have asserted their right to their own room to have both privacy and a chance to express individual tastes.[45] Being able to close the bedroom door or even to lock it gives teenagers a sense of independence and perhaps encourages them to pursue amusements forbidden by parents.

One of the strategies to accommodate children was the bunk bed, still useful as a way to stack sleeping children and capture more floor space. Bunk beds may even help young adults expand the capacity of small apartments, offering extra sleeping spaces for visiting friends. Zachary Fine, settling into his first adult apartment in 2016, chose an unusual bunk bed that provided a single mattress on the upper level and a full-size bed on the lower so he could have conversations with his pals when they stayed overnight.[46]

Twentieth-Century Bathroom and Bedroom Improvements

Later in the twentieth century residents who could afford one added a second bathroom, and by the early twenty-first century well-to-do home-buyers sought houses with a bathroom for every bedroom on the chamber floor and extra baths for other floors. Dressing rooms are supplied for each bedroom in costly new houses of the twenty-first century, and in master bedrooms some couples prefer "his-and-hers master bath suites," which may have double sinks, larger shower stalls, or saunas and exercise equipment.

Bathrooms become refuges, the only place in the house to get away from daily demands and distractions. Busy parents "want a place where they can think, where they won't be bothered. And there aren't a lot of places where that can happen," said the research director of the National Association of Home Builders.[47] In recent years, bedrooms and bathrooms have even incorporated some aspects of cooking and eating space, enabling some couples to enjoy a bathroom cocktail at the end of the day.[48]

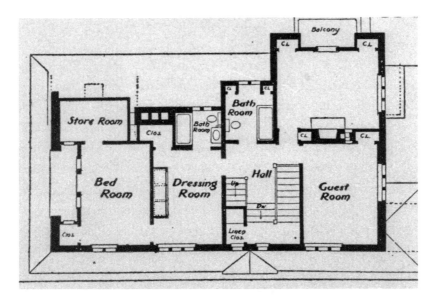

Fig. 62. A 1916 master suite includes the owners' bedroom, walk-in closets or dressing rooms, and a bathroom, sometimes two. Well-to-do twentieth-century owners wanted maximum privacy and convenience in their private quarters. The master bedroom often serves as a sitting room and a refuge from other members of the household. A luxury bathroom in the twenty-first century may contain a couch and a refrigerator, serving as a private place to enjoy cocktails. Plan of second floor in "a house designed for housekeeping," *Country Life in America* 29–30 (February 1916): 38.

New activities of the postwar years motivated an expansion of bedroom uses. In a *Better Homes and Gardens* 1956 article, "Ideas for a Double-Duty Room," the authors suggest that built-in furniture can transform just another bedroom into a TV room, a study, and a guest room. Adolescent sons and daughters have their own interests, as do older residents in the household such as grandparents.[49] To satisfy their unique needs, the proposed bed-sitting room has a complete set of bedroom furnishings at one end and a full sitting room with sofa, bookshelf, TV, and stereo at the other end. The "round-the-clock room" serves as a studio apartment for a self-sufficient son, daughter, or grandmother. A queen-size bed in the center of the room serves as a sofa in daytime, the headboard a storage unit and room-divider. This placement leaves space along the walls for diverse uses—a dining area, a conversation corner, a desk, and a rolling stereo cabinet. Shelf and drawer units at one end of the bedroom support books, the TV, and storage. Easy chairs and a table make a reading area. The fold-out sofa sleeps guests. "Draw draperies assure darkness for daytime televiewing." Bedrooms, which are normally associated with the dark, might be particularly well suited to the dark conditions recommended for viewing television in the 1950s.

In the 1960s, the idea of a "master suite" took hold among middle-class homeowners as a refuge in the house for stressed breadwinners, the husband and wife, who both worked outside the home.[50] "These days, more and more emphasis is being placed on the master bedroom." According to a 1964 *Better Homes and Gardens* article, creating a master suite requires adding a bathroom and a walk-in closet to the average-size bedroom. "Some have space for a king-size bed, some easy chairs or a couch, a desk, television and stereo equipment, plus one or two walk-in closets and a spacious, comfortable bathroom attached." The demands of rearing a family and the exertions of childcare might make parents long for a refuge, which the bedroom could provide. "When children invade the den and family room, Mom and Dad can steal away to their own quiet quarters in a bed-sitting room," suggested a 1953 article in *Better Homes and Gardens*.[51] In calling such arrangements "master suites," *Better Homes and Gardens* acknowledges that bedrooms have not just become places to sleep, but also places that "function as a kind of refuge—a decompression chamber" that is especially attractive to parents who both work.

"The multipurpose master bedroom is no longer an indulgence or a privilege enjoyed by people with space to spare," advised *Better Homes and Gardens*. Men working in postwar white-collar jobs found that they needed to bring office work home with them and secure a place where they could do this paperwork undisturbed.[52] With imagination, even a small bedroom can be shaped to accommodate an office area, a sitting area, and the bed and dressing area. In the work area, for the man who works at home, dark-finish furniture has a "masculine look," while the wall can be lined with compartmentalized stacking units to hold files and office machines. The sitting area has a fireplace and television, and a divider wall sets off the sleeping area. While the authors assert that adults need a bedroom retreat essential to rest in a fast-paced world, their recommendation to turn the bedroom into an office at home betrays rest.

Some couples who can afford the extra space elect to have separate bedrooms. A 1969 *House and Garden* article shows his and hers bedrooms for Mr. and Mrs. Harold Mertz, each of whom has a bed covered in upholstery fabric to pass as a sofa during the day. Mrs. Mertz's writing table "can, with the addition of a hair-dryer and beauty aids, be transformed into a little pampering room," while in Mr. Mertz's room two chairs with ottomans serve for relaxing or "doing paperwork." Still, most households cannot afford the extra space it takes to separate the married couple, nor do most married couples want to challenge the norm of a shared marital bedroom.

As house sizes expanded in the 1980s, the desire for such multi-purpose bedrooms increased, and size and layout of master bedrooms accommodated extra activities. What do women say about their bedrooms? *House and Garden's* Mary Seehafer invited women to give their opinions in a 1982 article. Mrs. A. L. Walker of New York thinks that women use their bedrooms more than any other room. "I absolutely live here! I write, sew, do needlepoint, watch television, and 'keep the home fires burning' from this all-important command post." Her bedroom is a penthouse room with a terrace, furnished with a large couch and lots of books. Mrs. Robert Kardashian represents her bedroom as "a little apartment—an afternoon retreat where I can make calls or write letters, and an evening place for my husband and me to read and relax alone." While the Kardashians' bedroom is represented as "hers," it seems that it is really the marital bedroom and thus "his" as well. This model of referring to the marital bedroom as *hers* has roots in the nineteenth century when the term "mother's room" named the marital bedroom. Yet according to Mrs. Kardashian her husband does not feel excluded, since he does like the ruffles and flourishes.[53]

In recent times, once-dedicated bedroom and bathroom spaces for prosperous householders have taken on some aspects of dining. Bedrooms incorporate mini-refrigerators and microwave ovens. Bathrooms also often include a "morning kitchen with mini-refrigerator and coffee maker," reported a recent *New York Times* article. Mary Jo Peterson, a Connecticut interior designer, felt that couples like to get away from their busy lives in an expanded bathroom where they can enjoy a cup of coffee in the morning or a glass of wine at night. Mark Meier of Houston said he and his wife usually eat breakfast in their master bathroom: "I introduced my wife to the concept of meals in the tub."[54] Even bathrooms "become a place of relaxation and refuge," incorporating not just bathroom fixtures but "a chaise lounge by the window . . . stereos and refrigerators to create . . . [a] festive sanctuary."[55]

The spaces for sleeping, bodily care, and other privacy-requiring spaces have expanded over the course of four centuries. In seventeenth-century one-room houses there was no dedicated interior space for sleeping or bodily care; instead, every space served as a place to sleep. Before privacy was even articulated as a need in houses, casual, ad hoc and often outdoor spaces at seventeenth-century single-room dwellings served sleeping needs and cleanliness requirements.

Housebuilders with ample resources created specialized bedrooms or chambers in eighteenth-century houses. By the mid-nineteenth century, mass-market design books assumed that all their readers would want one or more bedrooms. Those who could afford to focus on health made sure their bedrooms protected sleepers against dust, bedbugs, and poor ventilation. Bedrooms also guarded mental health in the form of clearly gendered furniture and decoration, certifying early twentieth-century children as boys and girls. Yet rural settlers of the nineteenth century and the poor of every era still slept wherever they could.

In the modern era, houses were marketed as "two-bedroom" or "four-bedroom," the number of bedrooms being a recognized measure of the size of a house. New houses produced for twentieth- and twenty-first-century lower-income markets almost always included at least two dedicated bedrooms and a three-fixture bathroom. In the expanding size of late twentieth-century suburban houses, several bedrooms could be large enough to serve as second living rooms.

Eighteenth- and nineteenth-century houses had dedicated a very small percentage of a house's square footage to bathing and toileting facilities. Expansive five-bedroom apartments in grand New York buildings of the 1880s provided only a single bathroom for tenants. By the early twentieth century, however, a three-fixture bathroom became standard for all classes in new dwellings. Later in the twentieth century, bodily care spaces took even more of a dwelling's square footage with extra bathrooms, walk-in closets, and dressing rooms. Private, bodily care spaces can sometimes occupy almost half an apartment's square footage in the early twenty-first century. In certain recently marketed expensive apartments and houses, bathrooms contain special types of showers, jacuzzi bathtubs, Japanese musical bidet-toilets, and even refrigerators, easy chairs, and spaces for cocktails or a light meal.

5

CIRCULATION, OR GETTING
FROM HERE TO THERE

In architecture, the term circulation is used to identify entrances, exits, and paths of movement used by people to get into and through spaces. There are numerous terms to designate elements of a house's circulation system: a walk or path, front steps or ramp, porch or veranda, colonnade, patio, front door or entrance, vestibule, entryway or lobby, foyer, hall, corridor or passage, stair-hall, staircase, back stairs, back door, side door or door from the garage. Houses also contain the circulation paths for water, heat, and other utilities, but here we will focus on how people circulate.[1]

Separate passages, halls, or corridors carry traffic from one part of the house to another, sometimes with polite ornament and generous processional spaces, sometimes merely plain, narrow, and functional. Stairs continue the circulation from one floor of the house to an upper or lower level. There are also circulation routes not through corridors or hallways, but across rooms typically used for something else—we'll call that a customary path of movement. For example, it is customary for people to walk through the kitchen to go out the back door.

To further complicate circulation, some paths of movement are set aside for only owners and their guests, while servants or service people will use different paths. In more formal eras people approaching a house from outside would follow specific circulation paths to arrive at their proper entrance—family and guests at the front door, tradesmen or workers at the side or back. In recent times with informal manners framing movements, family and friends may prefer to come in at the back door while the UPS man delivers at the front.

Finally, while circulation elements are designed to get people from here to there, they may also serve undesignated purposes. People may use the stairs not just to go up or down, but to sit on a landing and spy on others down below. The wide hallway that provided a graciously spacious

Fig. 63. This front door on the 1660s Jackson House in Portsmouth, New Hampshire, is defensive, sturdy. It conveys residents' desire for safety and protection in the early years of settlement. Photo E. C. Cromley.

entrance in one era may seem a waste of space to another set of inhabitants who would prefer to use the hall to bunk their many children. A door not only provides an opening to invite visitors in, but may also give a glimpse of an unwelcome visitor in time to lock him out.

Opening Doors

Anyone going into a house has to start at the door. Doors mark the place where people leave the outdoors and encounter the indoors, or leave one room to enter another. Some doors give a formal, ceremonial aspect to entering and some declare themselves purely utilitarian. Seventeenth-century householders typically thought of their doors as protective, even defensive, made of sturdy timber, unornamented. They were constructed on the front of the house, but the façade was not conceived of as symmetrical around a center entrance.

When American house-builders added symmetrical façades in the early eighteenth century, front doors received the most attention. The front door

Fig. 64a and Fig. 64b. Front doors have received special elaboration from the early eighteenth century to the present. Classical ornament has often been preferred, as seen on the 1758 John Paul Jones House in Portsmouth, New Hampshire. Pediments, pilasters, and moldings continue to announce the importance of the entrance, as on this twentieth-century public housing in Alexandria, Virginia. Photo E. C. Cromley.

declared itself the most important feature of the façade through its location on the center line and by its extra classical ornament. Window frames might be very simply formed with small molding elements, but doors often got wooden pilasters or columns, special glass beside or above the door opening, panels in the wood of the door itself, and sometimes a pediment above the door frame. In the nineteenth and twentieth centuries this importance continued through ornament. Many writers believed that the doorway reflected the taste of the house owner and told the passing public what kind of family lived there.[2]

Circulation among the rooms that the upper-middle-class household used was modulated by connecting doors between rooms. An eighteenth-century dining room arranged for entertaining would have a substantial, ornamented door from the central hall or passage for householders and their guests, but it would also have a lesser door connecting to the service stairs and kitchen so servants could deliver refreshments unobtrusively. The first Harrison Gray Otis house in Boston built in the 1790s by Charles Bulfinch has these features, as does the eighteenth-century Maryland house, Riverdale Park. The elaborate door from the entrance hall into the dining room

Fig. 65a and Fig. 65b. Through their level of ornament, doorways inside costly eighteenth- and nineteenth-century houses conveyed the rank of the people using them. The elaborated dining-room door at Poplar Hill in Clinton, Maryland, was used by guests and family members entering the room from the hall for a meal, while the plainer dining-room doorway was for the servants who delivered meals from the kitchen. Photo E. C. Cromley.

Fig. 66. Farnsworth House glass door, Plano, Illinois, 1950. The tradition that front doors should be symbolic of welcome and protection was reconceptualized by modernist architects such as Mies van der Rohe, who sometimes chose invisibility, blending a glass door with the glass walls around it. Photo E. C. Cromley.

hinted at the grandeur that awaited guests, while the plainer door for servants declared their lesser status.

In the twentieth century, the traditional function of a welcoming front door has sometimes been questioned. Frank Lloyd Wright's 1908 Robie House in Chicago has a "front" door relocated to the back of the house. A desire for privacy led Wright to conceal the main entrance to his design. The front doors of modernist houses may be made of glass, hardly distinguishable from the glass walls in which they are mounted, as in Mies van der Rohe's 1950 Farnsworth House in Plano, Illinois.

When attached garages became requirements for suburban houses, builders located them at the back or side of a house, but by the 1950s garages had become front-facing elements. People came home to their garages, stowed the car, and entered their houses through a door from the garage into the house. Often this door led into a mud room or laundry room, then to the kitchen. Entering householders avoided the formal parts of the house entirely. Nonetheless, front doors retain a lot of symbolic power, drawing the eye and standing both as a welcoming overture and as a guarantor of private interior space for the family, protecting them from strangers.

The simplest early American houses of one room have the simplest circulation: householders come in and out through the only door. All the interior space is laid out before the visitor; specific pieces of furniture may indicate different uses located in various areas of the one-room dwelling,

but no separate passageways lead from part to part. Instead of a purpose-built hall or corridor that would be employed in a larger building's plan, in the one-room house circulation paths reflect customary movement and convenience (see fig. 15) for a one-room house with just one door). A more complex circulation pattern with stairs has an additional purpose: circulation establishes a rank order of better and lesser spaces.[3] In a one-room house with a ladder to the sleeping loft, it is probably the children and/or servants who will sleep on the upper floor while master and mistress sleep on the main level.

If one enters a seventeenth-century, two-room house, one might first stand in a lobby, a very small but dedicated circulation space. Then movement choices need to be made: go left through one doorway and find yourself in the hall; or go right through another doorway and find the parlor or chamber; or go up the stair that rises from the lobby to a second floor. The Comfort Starr House in Guilford, Connecticut or the Boardman House in Saugus, Massachusetts (fig. 2) had such two-room plans in the seventeenth century (before enlargement through later additions).

Fig. 67. Two levels of front doors. In the era of attached garages, front doors on suburban houses decorate the front but may almost never be used. Access into the house through the garage is more convenient. However, ornamented front doors may still hold their symbolic value and provide welcoming images, as on this c. 2000 house near Friendship, Maine. Photo E. C. Cromley.

Confusingly, three distinct meanings for the word "hall" were in use during the seventeenth and eighteenth centuries. The principal or sometimes the only room in a house was called the "hall," from English tradition where a major house for a land-owning family was called "the hall"; remember that Robin Hood lived in a house named "Locksley Hall." But in later centuries the word "hall" typically meant a passage or corridor dedicated to circulation. Descriptions of houses in inventories sometimes clarify this confusion by naming the corridor "passage" instead of "hall," saving the name hall for a major room. An inventory for Bostwick House in Bladensburg, Maryland, prepared in 1785, gave the names of the ground-floor spaces: the large room, the dining room, the passage, and the back room, avoiding the word "hall" entirely.[4]

Even in one-room houses, residents might describe the path they traversed between the beds and living area on one end of the room and the kitchen on the other as a "hallway." Residents of one-room or single-pen houses in rural North Carolina were interviewed by folklorist Michael Ann Williams in the 1970s. Because of the customary way they traversed the space, they thought of their house as having a bedroom, a living room, a hall, and a kitchen—even though those were just zones in a single long room with no dividing walls.[5]

Eighteenth-Century Multi-Room Circulation

More differentiated circulation paths developed in larger eighteenth-century houses with several rooms. One type of elite plan, often named "Georgian," favored a central hall or passage that cut through the house front to back on all the principal floors. The 1715 Warner House in Portsmouth has a front door opening into this type of wide center hallway. Visitors entering at the front door saw several interior doors opening off the center hall as well as a stair rising to the second floor. Servants in upper-class houses guided visitors to the proper door and room. It suited well-to-do householders to have a preliminary space in which to separate different kinds of visitors and clarify their social rank. The center hall in these larger houses preserves owners' privacy by positioning the visitor to wait before a servant or resident invites him or her to penetrate further into the house.[6] Halls and stairs are essential utilitarian elements in houses but also provide a field for ornament and social interaction. Expert woodworkers built grand staircases that ornamented the center halls in larger

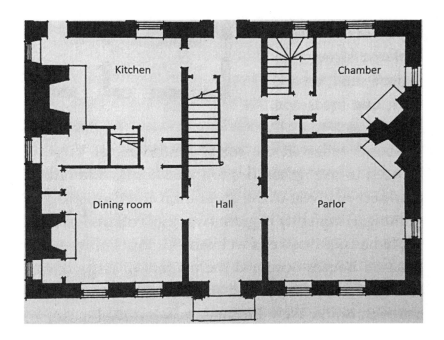

Fig. 68. A center-hall plan. Used in many eighteenth-century houses with multiple rooms, the center hall or passage provides an indoor space for visitors to be vetted. Here at the c. 1715 Warner House in Portsmouth, New Hampshire, servants or householders could discern whether a visitor was a social friend or a business contact or just making a delivery, and direct that person to wait in the hall or come on in.

eighteenth-century houses. Turned balusters in varied patterns caught the visitor's eye and reinforced the fact of the owner's prosperity.

Within elite eighteenth-century houses a population of servants and a population of family members shared spaces. To keep residents and servants on their proper tracks, separate servants' passages and stairs were built.[7] The second smaller stair seen in the Warner House plan indicates circulation for servants. Tradesmen and service people were directed to the rear door of such a house to do business with or deliver messages or goods to members of the household. When household workers were African American and house owners white, the pre-Civil War rule required separation of movement paths, both inside and outside the house. Historian Dell Upton has analyzed the servants' stairs and passages inside the house, then the paths within plantation landscapes, mapping African American paths of movement through the landscape whose meanings mirror the segregated halls and stairs within.

The hall or passage space was not just for circulation, but might also be the site of social exchanges. In his diary of the 1770s, Philipp Fithian recorded his experiences at the Virginia plantation owned by the Carter family. On a July Sunday, he observed an "old Negro man" waiting in the passage who had come to complain to Mr. Carter that he was not getting his promised peck of corn per week. "We were sitting in the passage, he sat himself down on the Floor clasp'd his hands together, with his face di-

Fig. 69. Servants' stair view. In grand eighteenth- and nineteenth-century houses, servants' stairs were typically narrower and more enclosed than the stairs used by residents and visitors. While servants had work to do that might have been facilitated by more generous paths of movement, they were also supposed to do their work invisibly, so their passages and stairs tended to be concealed. This servants' stair is pushed to the outside in the back of the c. 1860 Bellamy House, Wilmington, North Carolina. Photo E. C. Cromley.

rectly to Mr. Carter, and then began his narration."[8] Another eighteenth-century observer visited Tuckahoe, the Virginia home of the Randolph family, and described how the two main wings of the house were joined by central hall called a "saloon" that provided circulation space between the wings. This space had lots of doors and windows, and a high ceiling, so in addition to circulation it provided cool air in the "scorching and sultry heat of the climate." Men could even leave their wigs off when cooling themselves here.[9] Although circulation spaces always had the specific function of giving users paths of movement, they also often had additional socializing functions like these.

Nineteenth-Century Halls and Stairs

Circulation space was generously allocated in later nineteenth-century urban row houses designed for the elite. Characteristically four or five stories, row houses such as Boston's Gibson House required dedicated stairs and corridors for traveling from one floor to the next, from basement-level kitchens and service rooms to first- and second-floor reception and social rooms, third- and fourth-floor family bedrooms, and attic servants' quarters. The Gibson House had a stylish stair for family and visitors paired with a service stair for the first four levels. New York row houses typically attached this circulation pair of stair and corridor to the side wall on every floor. Some Philadelphia builders of row houses adopted an alternative location, building staircases perpendicular to side walls, which enabled them to act as a buffer between the front and back rooms on each floor. Boston builders usually chose the side-wall location in Back-Bay row houses developed in the second half of the nineteenth century.[10]

Over the decades of the nineteenth century, articles about building and decorating a home entrance hall agreed that it should give a visitor an introduction to the owner's taste and hint at the décor of the rest of the main rooms. The hall should maintain a dignified style in keeping with its role as partially public. In the Victorian period, according to historian Kenneth Ames, the hall's furnishings would have guaranteed a good first impression

Fig. 70. A hall stand at Coolmore Plantation, North Carolina. Later nineteenth-century middle-class entrance halls were the site for a stand holding coats, umbrellas, hats, and a mirror. Guests and owners could leave outerwear and check their appearance before going in or out. The hall stand could have a simple design or use more elaborate materials, indicating something of the householders' wealth and taste. Photo E. C. Cromley.

in middle-class houses. An important piece of hall furniture was the "hall stand," which held coats, hats, and umbrellas and provided a place to sit for a moment, a mirror to check your hat or hairdo, and a tray for leaving a visiting card. The stand's level of luxury and costliness of materials asserted the household's level of prosperity, or indeed claimed a higher level than the bank account would demonstrate.[11]

The amount of space taken up by row house stairs and halls was often criticized by contemporaries. What a waste of energy for the mistress and her servants to be climbing all those stairs all day long, they said. Furthermore, stairs can be a safety challenge and a site for falls if not well illuminated. A 1916 writer advised that long stairways in city houses probably needed artificial light, even during the day. Fortunately, newer types of house lighting were available and flexible: "the electric bulb and the gas pilot" allowed light to be provided and then turned off as needed.[12]

When urban row houses became too expensive for most single families in the mid-nineteenth century, either because of a household's diminished resources or due to rising real-estate costs, it was fairly easy for owners to convert row houses to boarding houses or separate apartments because of their well-developed circulation systems.[13] Each floor of a formerly single-family house could become a private apartment for a separate household, or two families might share a floor when they needed to save on rent. With the addition of several kitchens and baths, single-family row houses were transformed into multi-family apartment houses in dense American cities. Landlords rented one or a suite of rooms opening from the corridors that had once separated servants from family. Apartment-house designers focused on preserving privacy, not just among family members within apartments, but also between tenant households.

At the Riverside Buildings in Brooklyn, New York, housing reformer A. T. White experimented with a system of external circulation. Each apartment unit was accessed by an outdoor stair and a balcony or corridor. Because wind and rain reliably washed these circulation elements, the stairs would always be clean and the maintenance costs kept low. Interior circulation within the apartment unit kept halls to a minimum—units had only three rooms and utilized paths through rooms rather than consuming space and spending construction money on separate halls.

In northern New England a common multiple dwelling constructed especially by French Canadian builders was called the "block" type.[14] External circulation on stacked wooden porches gave access to varying-sized

CO-OPERATIVE HOUSEKEEPING IN TENEMENTS.

Fig. 71. Outdoor circulation for working-class tenants provided stair and balcony access to each household unit on the exterior. These were kept clean by rain and wind, allowing the managers to save money on maintenance. The Improved Dwellings Association design for buildings in New York used the device of outdoor circulation first developed for tenements in mid-nineteenth-century London, England. Drawing in Bisland, "Co-operative Housekeeping in Tenements," *Cosmopolitan* 8 (Nov. 1889): 35. Tenements on this model built at Hicks and Warren Streets, Brooklyn, by A. T. White.

apartments of two to seven rooms. Their characteristic circulation path brought tenants first into the kitchen, and then to the apartment's other rooms. Contrary to middle-class standards of pushing the kitchen to the rear of the plan and the main entrance nearest the social room to the front, these working-class householders used the kitchen as their principal social room as well as the location of the main entrance and circulation hub.

The boundary between public and private circulation space became a bewildering issue in the design of middle- and upper-middle-class apartment houses beginning in the 1860s. While most American city-dwellers seemed to prefer separate houses for individual families, then as now urban land was too expensive to support enough affordable dwellings. City residents turned to apartment buildings where elevators and stairs, large lobbies, and narrower halls or corridors on the several floors gave access to individual household units. Tenants disagreed whether an entrance lobby or stair should be read as private social space or should be understood as neutral public space.[15] Some argued that all the people who lived under one roof should treat each other with friendly greetings and hold conversations in the main lobby or on the stairs. Others insisted that one's own apartment unit was the only suitable terrain for social interaction and the rest of the building's shared spaces should be seen as akin to the public sidewalk where strangers respected each other's privacy and anonymity. Architects responded to these different notions of public vs. private circulation space by decorating their lobbies and stairs to encourage one interpretation or the other: those who wanted to encourage social interaction in the lobbies employed ornament and upholstered furnishings that looked like those in a parlor, while those who held to sidewalk neutrality for halls and lobbies used stark tile, hard surfaces, and benches that discouraged lingering.

Late Victorian houses for the elite made entering the house a special event. The first spaces that a visitor encountered in a sizable private house of the 1890s comprised a carefully planned sequence for entry. Visitors to the Charnley House in Chicago walked up three steps from the street to the wood and glass front door, ornamented with a metal grille. Inside lay a small vestibule with a tile floor and five more steps leading to a carved wooden inner door. Vestibules often sustained a public character associated with the sidewalk—hard surfaces and impersonal finishes suggested that the visitor

Fig. 72. Multiple halls at the 1880s Berkshire Apartments by architect Carl Pfeiffer. Builders made use of multiple halls to provide circulation in apartment houses. A public hall opens from the public stair and elevator, giving access to each household's front door. The public hall opens to a private hall inside the unit, giving access to individual rooms. Often a rear service hall, stair, and elevator provided routes for service workers. Most of the apartment's bedrooms have two entrances, yet many contemporary apartment bedrooms have only one door, preserving the privacy of household members from each other. *American Architect and Building News*, no. 397 (August 4, 1883).

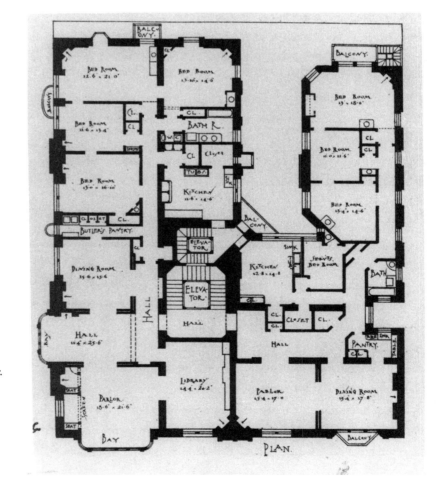

was in a liminal or borderline zone, not yet in the private space of the house. House owners could follow the recommendation of Charles Eastlake's influential book *Hints on Household Taste* (1870) that a hall be tiled in order to declare itself as still akin to exterior, public space—an interior space in which one was not yet inside.[16] Stepping through the inner front door into a reception hall should shift the visitor into private space that conveyed the overall decorative scheme of the house and, with it, the personality of the owner. The entrance sequence should occur in stages, rather than abruptly wrenching the visitor out of public space and into the private realm. Although the Charnley vestibule is small, it has this important function of buffering personal interior space from the sidewalk and street.

It would have been standard in well-to-do urban houses of the 1890s to have a separate reception space near the entrance door for messengers or tradesmen to wait in, or for visitors to remove their outdoor coats and boots. Furniture in this area was often comprised of straight-backed chairs without upholstery, so people knew not to spend any extra time there.[17] Advising his readers on how to finish such a reception room in 1888, architectural journalist William Peters warned against any conspicuous elements or jarring colors. "The introduction of any such incongruities would, in cultivated minds, excite comment similar to that caused by a showily or eccentrically dressed woman. Such comment would be ridicule, and what is so detrimental to the peace of a sensitive mind than this degrading possibility?"[18] In the reception room "we declare our taste to the world"; choose colors flattering to the mistress of the house, Peters advised. Women who want to check their appearance before going out will appreciate a mirror near the door. In their new Chicago house by Treat and Folz at Forty-Ninth Street and Drexel Boulevard, Mr. and Mrs. Martin Ryerson hung their reception room with pink silk held up by hooks and eyes to make it removable for cleaning. The silk was complemented by two large bearskin rugs on the wood floors.

Stair halls, while perhaps merely serviceable, might also have some of the charm of the interior rooms, wrote an 1880s advisor, Mary Gay Humphreys, in the *Decorator and Furnisher* magazine. She advised householders to have their hall built wider than usual and let it "serve some of the purposes of a sitting room." When an entrance hall includes "a certain number of the details of domestic life," it becomes more attractive. A long, straight staircase should be avoided if possible, wrote Humphreys, and instead have a stair interrupted by landings. Under the landing is extra space for a couch,

Fig. 73. Stair landings. Flights of stairs interrupted by landings were often featured in the entrance halls of larger houses, such as this one illustrated in Henry Hudson Holly's *Modern Dwellings*, no. 27 (1878). Landings provided a lookout position for viewers who wanted to see what was happening in the entrance hall below. In some households a stair overlook was enlisted to hold musicians at parties, or to feature the bride pausing to be admired as she descended the stairs at home weddings. In others, stair landings gave children a place from which to spy on their elders.

a small table, or a bookshelf. A few pictures could ornament the walls of the hall, but, opined a critic in 1883, "melancholy scenes of riot, suffering and murder, though they may be historical, are not calculated to create enlivening thoughts when one encounters them upon opening the front door."[19]

In the later nineteenth century, the stairs in the living halls of large houses served the added function of allowing for surveillance. French cultural historian Michel Foucault's study of the panopticon has alerted us to the place of surveillance in institutional buildings such as prisons; in the private house, surveillance was an opportunity rather than a requirement.[20] The living hall was often overlooked by a balcony from the stair landing, as in H. H. Richardson's Watts Sherman House in Newport, Rhode Island (1874–76), and Arthur Little's Shingleside in Swampscott, Massachusetts (1880–81) so that residents and visitors could monitor each other's movements. Residents' halls and stairs had breadth in contrast to servants' narrow stairs and halls. Servants didn't need to look around and see where people were—they had jobs to do and used circulation systems that kept them focused.

Stairs with broad landings also served additional purposes during entertainments at home. Brides gracefully descended the stairs for at-home weddings. People sat on the steps and put chairs on the landings to observe performances in the broad "living hall" at the base of the stairs. In 1898 Mrs. Glessner had platforms built upon her stairs so members of the Chicago Orchestra could be seated to play at her daughter's wedding.[21]

In her novel *A Backward Glance*, novelist Edith Wharton describes a young girl's memories of a party as seen from her perch on the top of the stairs: a "mild blur of rosy white-whiskered gentlemen, of ladies with bare sloping shoulders rising flower-like from voluminous skirts . . ."[22] The party, restricted to adults, still included this girl because the elevated stair landing gave her a secluded viewing platform from which to imagine herself in such a skirt at such a party.

Where raising children was the principal task of households in the post–World War II era, children's use of household circulation space might not be as intended. Staircases provided excellent perches for children observing the adults at parties and family celebrations. In Gillian Flynn's 2006 novel, *Sharp Objects*, the protagonist, Camille, has a troubled relationship with her chilly mother. Camille observes from her perch at the top of the stairs her mother and her mother's friends cooing over a visiting baby. As her mother cuddles the baby "ferociously," Camille "looked down from above like a spiteful little god . . . imagining how it felt to be cheek to cheek with my mother." What child did not observe a forbidden kiss, overhear a disagreement among relatives, or catch a glimpse of Santa assembling a last-minute gift from their seat on the stairs?[23]

Shrinking Twentieth-Century Circulation

The many types of hall in smaller early twentieth-century houses were listed in a 1908 *House Beautiful*: "Entrance-hall, stair-hall, reception-hall, living-hall, or just plain 'hall.'"[24] Architects of early twentieth-century houses worked to achieve the hospitable welcome found in large houses but using smaller square footage. Middle-class dwellers who could not afford a library or a drawing room might call their entrance room a "living hall" where they combined "the functions of a reception hall and a sitting room."[25] This living hall can have an open stairway rising from it, but it will have doors that preserve privacy by closing off the dining room and the kitchen beyond. Cozy, built-in inglenook seating near a fireplace could shield inhabitants from view of the front door or the stairs. The architects of these living halls believed that they would propagate "family fun . . . substantial leisure" and "become an inspiration to interesting living."[26]

Middling houses in the 1910s and 1920s used the most economical circulation strategies on the ground floor of two-story houses. Entry from the front door into a hall revealed a stair on one side and a living room on the other, no separate vestibule. This space might have room for a coat rack or perhaps a little coat closet that enabled the shift from outdoors to in. From the entrance, a visitor could move into the living room or proceed straight down the hall into the kitchen and the back door beyond, or go up the stairs to the bedroom level. When the house had a cellar, its door and stairs could be found along this hall as well. A 1911 description of a small family house explained how the stair hall became part of the space of the living room. The author, an architect, called her room a "living hall" since it combined the functions of a sitting room and a reception hall, and since it was linked to an open staircase, causing it to "pulsate . . . with life."[27] What child could resist chasing a brother or sister round and round the simple circulation path from hall to kitchen to dining room to living room, ad infinitum?

Advice columnists disagreed as to the best way to manage entering a modest-sized house. *House Beautiful* promoted combining the hall and the living room as a good way to economize, especially suitable to warm climate houses or informal vacation spots. But in chilly New England, for example, one might prefer a dedicated living room that is sequestered and cozy. In southern climates the hall cuts through the house, open both front and back, and is used as an informal sitting room to catch the breezes.

But other critics felt that "Nothing could be more inappropriate" than having a house's entrance open directly into the main living room.[28] For these early twentieth-century commentators, the entrance hall must protect the family's more personal space from anyone entering the house; they also suggest that the young, courting-age members of the household wanting to snuggle on the couch should be allowed more privacy than they would enjoy in the traffic of a combined circulation hall and living room.

In the 1910s, a butler's pantry was still a circulation element leading from kitchen to dining room and was standard in middle-class houses, even modest ones; but by the late 1930s it was disappearing. In households with servants, the route from kitchen to dining room was through the pantry, and it was traversed by servants carrying meals to guests at the dining table and used dishes and glassware back to the pantry for cleaning. In households where the housewife did this work, she served the meals and cleaned up, using the pantry on her route from dining room to kitchen. The butler's pantry controlled the flow of traffic, smells, and sounds of kitchen labor to protect the dining room; it also stored utensils, food and fuel, silverware, glassware, and dishes. Housework reformers like Christine Frederick as well as plan vendors and house-kit manufacturers argued that traversing the pantry required extra steps and that the most housework-efficient arrangement would have dining rooms immediately adjacent to kitchens.[29] They suggested eliminating the traditional pantry, or pantries—since some houses had more than one—substituting built-in or purchased cabinets to be located right in the kitchen.

Privacy or Convenience in Modern Circulation?

Although it seems contrary to the effort to make the modern kitchen efficient, traffic into and out of the house must often pass through kitchens to reach rear and side doors. The kitchen itself at the beginning of the twentieth century was normally clearly separated from the other rooms of the house but highly accessible through the use of multiple doors. At Frank Lloyd Wright's servant-run 1902 Willitts house the kitchen has a door into the butler's pantry and thence to the dining room, another door to the back stairs and thence to the rear service yard, and a third door that leads to the front entrance and reception rooms of the house. The kitchen is buffered from view by a double door at the front entrance side, which assures that smells from the kitchen will not escape into the living areas. To see into the kitchen, a guest would have to make a deliberate effort, passing through several doors, and would never inadvertently peer into this work zone.

In her 1912 book *Handbook of Housekeeping*, Isabel Bevier proposed a much more modest kitchen run by the housewife, not servants. Bevier's kitchen had three doorways: one opened to a back entry and rear porch;

Fig. 74. Small house plan using bathroom as circulation. Purveyors of modest-budget houses in the 1910s and 1920s such as the Aladdin Company were able to save on square footage by cutting dedicated circulation. In this bungalow plan with no separate halls or corridors, the only circulation to the bedrooms was through the bathroom, or through doors linking bedrooms to either kitchen or living room. Kitchens commonly contained multiple doors. In spite of home economists warning that kitchens should not be subject to traffic, they often became circulation hubs. This one has a door to the entry and cellar, to the pantry, to the porch, and to the dining room. *Small Houses of the 1920s.*

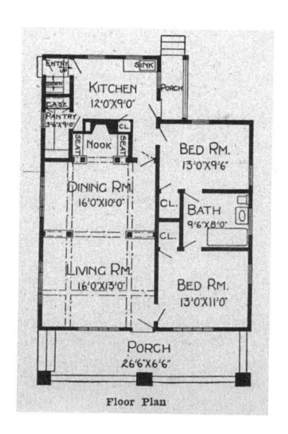

Floor Plan

one opened to a dining room; and a third was an exterior door into the ice-box which allowed the ice deliveryman to insert blocks of ice from outdoors. There is a seemingly obvious conflict in the function of the kitchen as both a portal to the outdoors and a machine for cooking in, yet this continued for decades in private houses. Bevier's kitchen, like Frank Lloyd Wright's, was protected from the more social front of the house, opening into a back entry-way and into the dining room but not into a living room. From the entrance hall of her house one had to pass through a hall door to get to the kitchen door. This kitchen was still sequestered at the back of the house even though it was no longer for servants but instead the space for the housewife.

Similar circulation is found in farm houses. In the 1915 Oscar Borass farmhouse in Lac Qui Parle, Minnesota, the kitchen occupied a large room with several doors: one led to the back porch and entry, one led into a pan-try, one led to the dining room, the fourth led to the entry hall and thence to the front porch, and yet a fifth door led to the basement stairs. One also reached a staircase to the upper floor from the kitchen. This kitchen was thus a major circulation hub pierced by six doors.

In working-class dwellings the kitchen's door to the outside was often the one most commonly used by inhabitants as the major entrance to the house. As historian Kingston Heath shows in his study of usage in Rhode Island triple-deckers (three unit apartment buildings, one household per floor), not just family members but close friends always used the back door and entered directly into the kitchen. If anyone chose the front door as the appropriate entrance, householders could tell that they were strangers.[30] The kitchen had four doors (from rear hall, interior stairway, broom closet, and pantry) as well as one wide opening into an adjacent sitting room. Circulation paths, as they were developed by the users in the triple-decker, created apparent conflicts with the house plan's intended movement patterns.

The kitchen served as a major circulation hub for the back of the house and exposed its users to heavy traffic. To compensate for the inconvenience of extra kitchen traffic, many of the kitchen appliances were moved into the pantry. This pantry-kitchen conformed to the earlier home economists' view that all extraneous traffic be kept out of the kitchen—accomplished by having only one door. Associating food with sociability belongs to an early American tradition of hospitality, but incorporating social life into the kitchen is more recently familiar from the history of late nineteenth- and early twentieth-century working-class families in tenements.

Like kitchens, dining rooms occupied an essential location in the circulation map of the house. In upper-middle-class houses of the early twentieth century, separate circulation paths buffered the outdoors and main entrance from the dining room and living room, just as separate hallways also preserved the privacy of bedrooms. But householders who could not afford to have separate access to every room in the house used the dining room as the customary circulation path from the front to the back of the house. The builder of the house at Florence Avenue in Buffalo, New York, a lower-middle-class double or two-family house, saved on square footage by combining essential circulation with the dining room. From the double parlor or living room at the front, one walked through the dining room to get to the kitchen, to a bedroom, and to a small corridor that led to further bedrooms and bath.

Circulation paths in designated halls and corridors that had been common in the nineteenth century were superseded by the modern architects' new favorite—flowing space. In 1948 the magazine *Architectural Forum* published a special issue of modern houses. The forty illustrated houses

Fig. 75. Dining rooms had to serve as circulation paths in middle- and working-class houses of the early twentieth century when no separate circulation was provided. In this c. 1905 double- or two-family house in Buffalo, New York, the dining room is the only route to the kitchen, two bedrooms, and the bathroom, while the kitchen is the only route to the back door and the rear stairs, which gave access to both the cellar and the upper unit. While front and rear stairs take up significant space, major savings were accomplished by omitting all other dedicated circulation except for a very short hall between dining room and kitchen. Drawing by SUNY-Buffalo students; in author's collection.

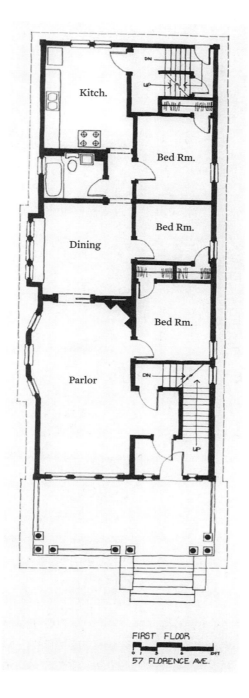

ranged from expensive ones with maids' rooms to quite low-budget ones, but their circulation patterns were similar in making the social rooms open to each other. Bedrooms and bathrooms still had doors and were reached from halls or corridors, but dining areas, living rooms, entrance lobbies, and even some kitchens were no longer enclosed.

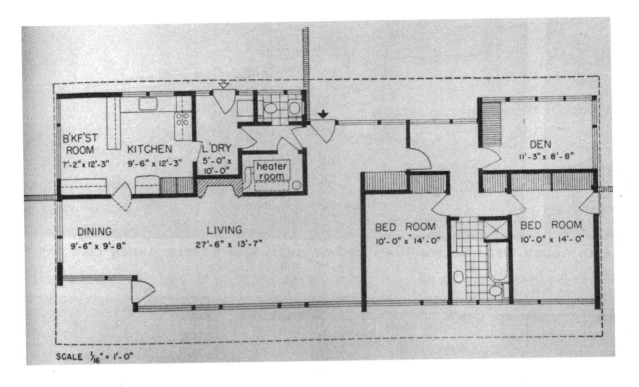

Fig. 76. Modern open plans needed no halls or corridors for the more social parts of the house; however, builders did supply enclosed bedrooms and bathrooms with hallway access and a single door per room, since users of bedrooms and bathrooms still valued privacy. House 6, by architects V. Furno and J. Harrison, 1948, Brookville, NY. "40 Houses," *Architectural Forum* 88 (April 1948): 101.

Visitors to these modern houses would typically encounter only a modest framing of an entrance space. From the front door, house 35 has a small lobby area with a coat closet and folding doors protecting the view into a living room on the right. But more typically, as at houses 18, 20, and 31, the visitor enters more directly into the living room with only a coat closet to buffer further views into the house. The unbuffered, direct entrance into the living room is common in lower-middle-class developers' housing as in the Cape-style houses at Long Island's Levittown, so having an entrance area set apart a bit would signify that the owners aspired to a more elevated social class.

Builders of small bungalows in the early twentieth century tried to minimize the square footage of their houses while maintaining the convenience of privacy-protecting circulation paths. They developed an ingenious design that reduced the space of separate circulation by having visitors and householders enter directly into a living room. The living room opened through a wide door frame into a dining room, and a door from dining room into kitchen led finally to the back door. They needed a separate hall only in the private zone of the house—the bedrooms and bathroom. A convenient bungalow hall was reduced to a mere twenty square feet or so, yet from this hall one had separate doors into two bedrooms and a bathroom. Some builders even incorporated the bathroom into the circulation path, so that one moved from one bedroom to the second by using the bathroom itself as a passage. This plan put bathroom privacy at risk with its two doors but saved yet more square feet by eliminating the hall.

Opposite to the open-plan flow of customary circulation through the social spaces in modern houses, the bedroom and bath zone preserved closed rooms. In twenty-first-century houses bathrooms are often provided for each bedroom, and the bathroom entrance is part of the bedroom suite. Preserving halls and doors in the bed and bath zone reinforced privacy and individual territory.

Passages, corridors, hallways—interior circulation spaces—have been thought about in three different stages. In early houses people moved to and through one or two rooms along customary routes; they got from part to part by simply passing through interior spaces, regardless of each area's intended function. In the next stage of multi-room houses, builders provided specific circulation paths such as lobbies, hallways, passages, corridors, and stairs to frame and direct people's movement and protect the specific functions and privacy of separate rooms. More recently a late twentieth-century combination of these concepts has responded to people's sense of what elements are properly private and what should be more public and shared within a house. Ground-floor, open-plan, living-kitchen spaces invite non-directed general circulation, distinct from a wing or separate floor where well-defined private halls and corridors lead to protected individual bedrooms and bathrooms.

6

STORAGE

Dwellers need the house and its nearby landscape to store the things that they are not using. Storing items in prosperous households with numerous possessions requires many more hooks, shelves, and closets than are needed by poorer folks with few possessions. Availability of goods changes radically with the era, so even if you belonged to a wealthy household in the eighteenth century, you couldn't need as much storage as your middling counterpart in the twenty-first century who had access to industrially produced goods, well-stocked stores, and Amazon. Specific kinds of goods are often given storage built for the purpose: clothing in bedroom closets, shovels on hooks in the shed, cars stored in the garage. But the rhythm in which things are used varies greatly according to the category of things, the season, and the economy in which a particular household participates. Cooking tools might be used every day, perhaps several times a day, by cooks of all classes and in every geographical location. But only in chillier climates would you need a warm coat, and it would only come out of storage when cold weather demanded. And for those without the means to have purpose-built storage, outdoor spaces around the homescape accommodate extra stuff.

Storage of Foodstuffs

Purpose-specific storage spaces originated with the need to store food. New Englander Samuel Symonds commissioned a house in Ipswich, Massachusetts after 1638. He instructed his builder to give him a first-floor room heated by a fireplace at each end, leaving it up to the builder to decide whether or not to put in a partition. Symonds did not care whether he had one room or two; rather, his primary focus was to ensure that the second floor would be strong enough to serve as a storehouse for corn. Col. Thomas Pettus's Virginia plantation house complex, lived in c. 1640–1690, had a dwelling house comprised of a large hall with an attached kitchen wing. The kitchen had a cellar to store foods needing a cool environment with additional food-storage structures on the nearby grounds—a dairy and a smokehouse. James Claypoole constructed a three-room house in Philadelphia in 1683 with a cellar in which he planned to store wine. A cellar to store wine, a second floor to store corn, or separate structures to store meat and dairy—their needs to store food motivated early settlers to include designed-for-the-purpose storage elements in seventeenth-century American houses.[1]

In the centuries before refrigeration, householders had to find ways of preserving food so it would not spoil after it was harvested. Dug into the earth near a house, a root cellar took advantage of the stable temperature of the earth to help preserve food. A room carved out of the ground might be strengthened by brick, stone, or wooden supports with a layer of earth sealing the top. Housewives stored vegetables from the end of one growing season to the next harvest on shelves, in barrels, and other containers. Eggs, too, were preserved, nested in layers of straw or paper. Houses with cellars

Fig. 77. People who had the means to create a vaulted cellar below a house created a cool atmosphere similar to a root cellar. This vaulted cellar at Belair, an upper-class, eighteenth-century house in Maryland, stored foods in barrels between the end of one growing season and the harvest of the next. Photo E. C. Cromley.

Fig. 78. Spring water was directed through a stone channel in the cellar of the Christian Ley House (c. 1750) on his Tulpehocken, Pennsylvania, farm. To keep foods and drinks cool, owners placed waterproof containers in the running water. When the flow reached the outdoors, they grew watercress in the resulting pond for food. Drawing by Charles Bergengren, 2002, in *Architecture and Landscapes of the Pennsylvania Germans*, 1720–1920 (VAF Guidebook, 2004): 48.

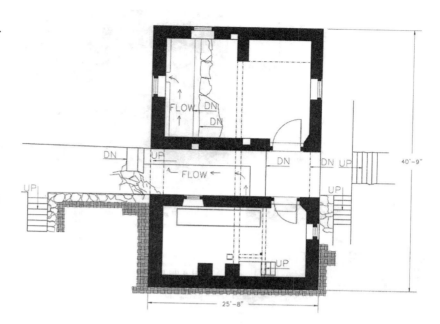

likewise made use of stable underground temperatures to store some of their food supply. Cellars with vaulted roofs, such as one at eighteenth-century Belair in Maryland, provided good cool storage for barrels of foods. In houses with sufficient space, food items were stored in several parts of the house in boxes and barrels. The 1720s inventory of the Virginia house, Bacon's Castle, lists the food-storage containers used in the cellar, on the ground floor, and in the attic.[2]

Dairy products needed a cool storage place such as the dairy at Eyre Hall, illustrated in chapter 1. Dairies for milk-related foods could be dug partly below ground to take advantage of cooler temperatures. In the eighteenth and early nineteenth centuries the cool temperature was sometimes provided by running water, such as a stream or spring, in an underground room. For households with extra resources, ice could be imported and stored below ground in an ice-house. With this convenience, elite households such as George Washington's served ice cream to eighteenth-century guests.

Meats also needed to be preserved and stored to keep them from spoiling. Some households possessed a smoke house, a freestanding small building in

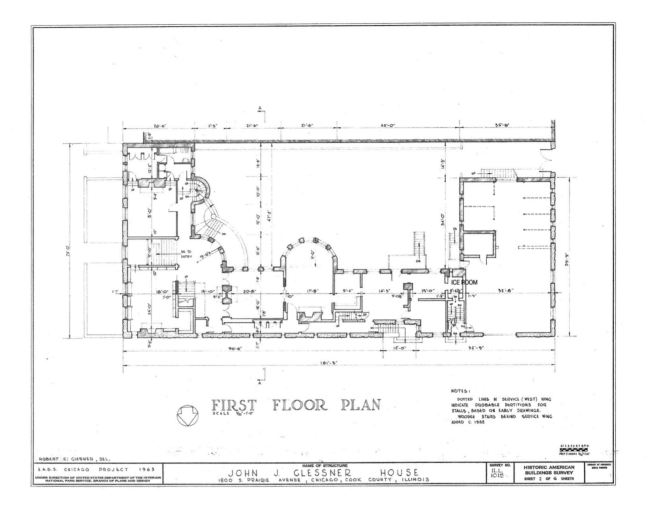

FIRST FLOOR PLAN
SCALE 3/32"=1'-0"

NOTES:
DOTTED LINES IN SERVICE (WEST) WING
INDICATE PROBABLE PARTITIONS FOR
STALLS, BASED ON EARLY DRAWINGS.
WOODEN STAIRS BEHIND SERVICE WING
ADDED C. 1938.

ROBERT C. GIEBNER, DEL.

H.A.B.S. CHICAGO PROJECT 1963
UNDER DIRECTION OF UNITED STATES DEPARTMENT OF THE INTERIOR
NATIONAL PARK SERVICE, BRANCH OF PLANS AND DESIGN

NAME OF STRUCTURE
JOHN J. GLESSNER HOUSE
1800 S. PRAIRIE AVENUE, CHICAGO, COOK COUNTY, ILLINOIS

SURVEY NO.
ILL.
1015

HISTORIC AMERICAN
BUILDINGS SURVEY
SHEET 2 OF 6 SHEETS

LIBRARY OF CONGRESS

which cuts of meat, brined or rubbed with salt and spices, would be hung from the ceiling. Under them a fire burning for several days surrounded the meat with smoke and heat to cure it. Cured meat could be stored in the smoke house until it was needed. Others constructed a brick chamber inside the house that extended out from one of the fireplace chimneys in the attic or adjacent to the kitchen. The same smoking and storage of meats took place in this interior smoke chamber.

Archaeologists have found various items stored in holes in the floor or in the ground in eighteenth- and nineteenth-century houses of the poor. African American educator Booker T. Washington described the cabin he occupied as a boy in the 1860s on a Virginia plantation in his 1901 autobiography, *Up from Slavery*. It was a typical log cabin with an earthen floor, about fourteen by sixteen feet, in which he lived with his mother, his brother, and his sister. In

Fig. 79. To store and chill their foods at the 1887 Glessner House in Chicago, the clients had their architect, H. H. Richardson, improve on an ice-box with a whole ice-room. Photo E. C. Cromley.

the center of the floor there was "a deep opening covered with boards, which was used as a place in which to store sweet potatoes during the winter."[3]

By the mid-nineteenth century, refrigerators (also called ice-boxes) offered another place to store foods that needed to be kept cool. The early refrigerators were insulated, ventilated boxes made of wood or metal. Large blocks of ice kept in an ice compartment were surrounded by shelves for food storage, and weekly ice deliveries were common in larger towns and cities. In Chicago, the Glessner House of 1886 incorporated kitchen storage in a sequence of pantries and an ice-room. Expanding on the idea of an ice-box, the Glessners had a whole room to which blocks of ice were delivered.

When electric motors became available to power household machines in the 1920s, electric refrigerators improved the capabilities for safe food storage in middling and upper-class electrified houses. Some rural households had access to commercial scale refrigerators and freezers invested in by agricultural collectives, and there they enjoyed storing their personal food portions long before urban and suburban customers could purchase a home-sized freezer.

Dining Storage

Just as any food surplus must be stored to keep it safe—from spoilage, animals, or insects—so too must the tools for eating that food—china, silverware, glass—be stored to be kept clean and safe. While poorer households did not have sets of china or plate in the eighteenth century, the well-to-do liked to show off their fine china and silver in purpose-built storage units. Located inside parlors or dining rooms, shelves or cupboards created for storing food-service items were also display units, decorative elements that conveyed the household's high status.

Eighteenth-century china closets were often built in beside the projecting brick mass of a dining-room fireplace, filling up the extra space on both sides. Shelves in these closets were often cut with a decorative profile. When there were glass panes in the upper half of the china-closet door, they allowed visitors and owners to admire collections of china, glass, and plate; plain storage containers occupied the lower part of the closet behind the solid parts of the door.

Gustav Stickley's early twentieth-century magazine *The Craftsman* promoted various ideas for built-in storage furniture to aid in food preparation and service. To make a separate dining room more efficient, the magazine

recommended a china cupboard built into the wall between kitchen and dining spaces. This cupboard would have doors opening into both rooms, so dishes could be put away after washing them in the kitchen, and removed from the other side to set the dining-room table. This idea saved the housewife extra steps. Stickley's house plans for a bungalow published in October 1912 illustrated a dining-room window seat with built-in china closets at each end of the window. The closet doors were all glass so guests could admire the china collection as well as the outdoor view, and under the window seat were three "capacious drawers."[4] Another bungalow from February 1915 made use of a combined dining-living room that was thirty-six feet long. Built-in cabinetry acted as a room divider in which one shelved china on the dining-room side and books on the living-room side. The same issue of the magazine gave plans for a bungalow whose food axis included a breakfast room, a kitchen, and a dining room. The kitchen featured built-in cabinets and an early ice-box called a "cooler," while the dining room was improved with a built-in buffet that had drawers below and glass-fronted shelves above a serving surface.[5]

Fig. 80a and Fig. 80b. An eighteenth-century china closet at Maple Hill Farm in Norwich, Vermont, both stored and displayed fine china and other dining implements. The closet has a glass panel in the upper part of the door to make fine possessions visible, placed on shelves that had decorative profiles. Below the glass panels, plain boxes and other containers for goods not on display were stored. Photo E. C. Cromley.

Kitchens had little or no cabinet space in the nineteenth and early twentieth century; equipment storage was all allocated to the pantry. Pantry functions and layout were well established according to magazine articles published in the early twentieth century—the pantry functioned as a china closet and a serving room.[6] Pantry builders were cautioned to preserve an unimpeded counter space by lifting the upper cabinets well above the counter so there would be room to place plates for serving or clearing the table. Servants washed dishes and glassware in the pantry sink. Advice was given on creating the correct spacing for shelves: measure one's china pieces to make sure each piece fits in its specific place. Pantry drawers held table linens, while cupboards stored table leaves. In elaborate households where a butler was employed, pantries also contained an ice-box. If the pantry and dining room were on another floor from the kitchen, pantries were linked to the kitchen with a dumbwaiter.

Fig. 81. A two-pantry house. Architects Raeder, Coffin, and Crocker designed this 1891 house with two pantries. One opens from the kitchen for storage, and the second one—a butler's pantry—links the kitchen with the dining room. The butler's pantry is not only the place where china, glassware, and other dining-room essentials were cleaned and stored, but it is also part of the circulation path. House designed for Evanston, Illinois, published in *Inland Architect* 18, no. 2, n.p.

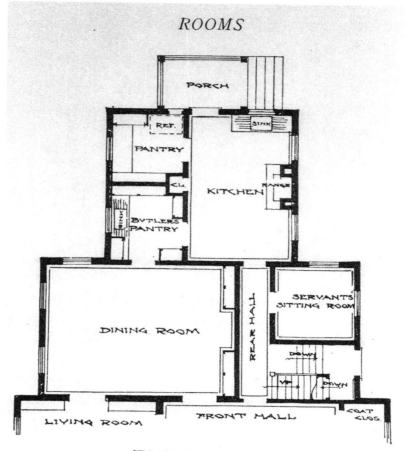

ROOMS

FIRST FLOOR PLAN

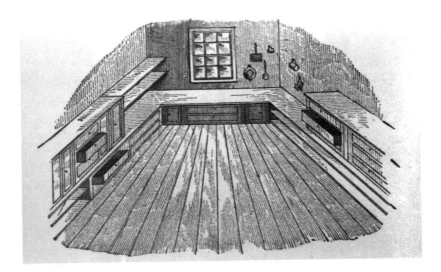

Fig. 82. In the 1880s, built-in pantry counters and cabinets, rather than cabinetry in kitchens, organized the storage of cooking and dining equipment. This drawing shows an ideal pantry of the 1880s. "A Well-arranged Pantry," *Household Conveniences* (New York: Orange Judd Co., 1884), 132.

Fig. 83. View of a nineteenth-century pantry with china on its shelves, in an 1888 house in Quincy, Illinois (architects Patton and Fisher) now used by the historical society. Adjacent to the kitchen, the pantry provided shelves for china and glassware, by then plentifully available through industrial production and distribution by railroad. The kitchen stove is visible beyond the pantry door. Not until the 1910s and 1920s did economical kitchens absorb those pantry shelves and look more like the built-in counters and cabinets that are so common for most kitchens today. Photo E. C. Cromley.

A 1915 *Country Life in America* reported on the refinement of food preparation and storage spaces in an expensive kitchen wing added to an old house near Chicago. The new wing contained the kitchen proper, a large serving pantry, a cook's pantry, a rear hall, and the back stairs. In the serving pantry were a double sink and cupboards for storing china, glass, silver, and linen. The cook's pantry contained storage barrels and cupboards for all food staples, and yet another sink. A broom closet contained space for storing table leaves, vacuum cleaner hoses, and other cleaning utensils and materials.[7]

Some upper-middle-class houses of this era had additional separate rooms connected to the kitchen, which broke down the general pantry storage into specific purposes such as individual food and equipment storage closets, and even safes for silver. In the expensive Boyce House in Chicago (see chapter 2), which was designed by architect Francis Whitehouse in the 1890s, the kitchen included a butler's pantry, a store room, two additional closets, and a special space for the ice-box in the kitchen's rear entry.

You will have noticed that the attributes of the turn-of-the-century pantry are the same as those we would expect to find in a mid-twentieth-century kitchen. How did all those pantry countertops and cabinetry transfer into the modern kitchen? High-budget, architect-designed houses retained their pantries through the early decades of the twentieth century, which suited servant-run households. It was at the low-budget end that pantries were phased out and kitchens supplied with pantry-style cabinetry.

Inexpensive houses with maximized efficiency were promoted by home economists in the 1910s and 1920s. They argued against pantries because they wasted the housewife's steps, and they also tended to become jumbled. Their research in domestic science led them to propose kitchens as small as possible with storage carefully planned in the kitchen. They recommended storing all the kitchen tools in shelves and cabinets there instead of in a pantry (see Isabel Bevier's small house plan, fig. 13, in chapter 1).

Rule-breaking architect Frank Lloyd Wright designed a kitchen for the 1904 Darwin Martin house in Buffalo, New York, working with a huge budget. He eliminated a separate pantry and unified the kitchen appliances within a framework of continuous countertops and built-in cabinets, which also hinted at the changes in kitchens to come. Perhaps Mrs. Martin asked him to leave out the separate pantry and storage closets common in well-to-do kitchens at that time. When looking at Wright's designs for summer cottages and more informal dwellings in the first decade of the twentieth century, one also notices missing pantries and built-in cabinetry shifted to kitchens.[8]

By the late 1940s both architect-designed and popular house kitchens in magazines or catalogs generally had absorbed the fitted cabinets that once belonged in the pantry. Formerly freestanding, separate sinks, stoves, and refrigerators were incorporated into this unified design. Countertops at a uniform height and cupboards below and above the counter omitted dirt-catching gaps. At the high end, the Darwin Martin house kitchen with its continuous counter surfaces and cabinetry seems about forty years ahead of the general run of elite kitchen design. At the low-budget end, 1910s home

Fig. 84. Smooth, continuous planes produced by matching storage units contrasted the modern kitchen with its predecessor. The discontinuous arrangement in 1910s kitchens was replaced in most post–World War II new houses with the counters and rows of upper and lower cabinets seen in this 1998 kitchen. Photo E. C. Cromley.

economists' kitchens presaged kitchens of today by incorporating all the storage once separated in pantries.

By the 1940s new kitchens in towns and cities, across classes, had the full array of electric appliances, plumbing, hot and cold water, and built-in storage cabinets that were once only accessible to the wealthy. Many modern houses lacked basements, so there was no food-storage room in the cellar as there had been in the past—perishable foods were all stored in the electric refrigerator.

Streamlined built-in storage furniture made the kitchen the one truly modern-looking room in houses that otherwise were often decorated in traditional styles. New appliances in modern materials stressed machine-like surfaces. Ranges, water supplies, and sinks were incorporated into the smooth countertop surface, so as not to disrupt the top and front planes of the built-in cabinets. Aesthetically there is a marked difference between the disjunctive elements seen in early twentieth-century kitchens and the smooth continuous line of the modern kitchen in the postwar years.

Clothes Storage

Householders in the colonial period did not shy away from display in general—they created china closets to show off their dining equipment—but clothes were not items to show independent of the body. While less prosperous people did not have any extra clothes, those who did needed to store them safely. Clothes in the eighteenth century were kept in storage chests or case furniture such as cupboards with shelves. These containers did not make clothing visible; it was hidden until the wearer decided to go out in the garment and be seen. Unlike textile decorations for rooms—upholstery, curtains—which are often all on display at the same time, items of clothing are always worn in rotation instead of all at once.[9]

The storage chests of the colonial period often had attractive ornament which called attention to the storage unit itself even as it concealed what was stored within. Painted and carved chests stored valued possessions, often textiles. Sometimes the initials or name of the chest's owner linked the stored goods with a particular person. Celebrating stored goods in decorated chests contrasts with later clothes closets that seek anonymity behind simple doors in the same plane as walls.

Clothes closets appear only sporadically in the rooms of eighteenth-century houses for the elite. The original concept of a closet is a small, private room, a den, or a study. Samuel Sewell, the New England diarist, wrote about a fire in his closet in the early eighteenth century where he had left a candle burning on his desk. In the American colonial period we see this type of little room at Stratford, the Lee home in Virginia, of the mid-eighteenth century. On the ground floor, several of the rooms have a small, windowed closet to be used as a private study. But in the modern definition, closets are small rooms used for storage.

The clothes closets provided by builders and architects in the eighteenth and nineteenth centuries were inconsistent in number and size. Some bedrooms had two closets while others in the same house had none; meanwhile, still others had a large dressing room in which clothes were both stored and put on. This unpredictable number of clothes closets suggests that many people were still content to store their clothes in chests or other case pieces. It also reflects the supply of clothes in the period: people had far fewer clothes in their wardrobes than they would have after mid-nineteenth-century industrial production increased the supply.

The inconsistent size and proportions of clothes closets in the eighteenth century continued for another century. The Woodlands in Philadelphia, built in 1747 and altered in 1788, had a second floor with eight bedrooms. Two of these had triangular clothes closets; two had deep narrow closets; two had small niches in the wall—not proper closets; and two bedrooms

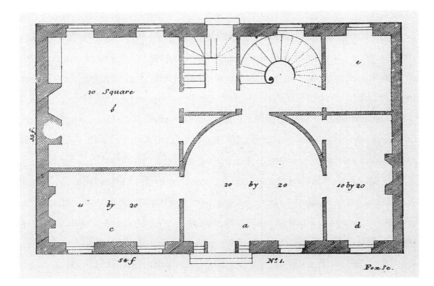

had no closets. The Swan House in Dorchester, Massachusetts had three bedrooms on the main floor, but only one had a clothes closet. Benjamin Henry Latrobe's Van Ness House in Washington, DC is an early example of a house with well-closeted bedrooms. Of the six bedrooms in the Van Ness House, two have relatively large, deep closets; one has two shallow closets; two have attached dressing rooms with windows; one has a triangular closet tucked in behind the curve of the main staircase; and one has no built-in storage.

Instead of being shaped and dimensioned for the care of clothes, most eighteenth-century closets seem to be sized opportunistically to fit into leftover architectural spaces. Triangular closets often fill in the space between the back of a squared room and an adjacent curved space such as a stair or the apsidal end of an adjacent room. Long, deep closets give poor access to clothes that were probably hung from pegs. Shallow closets parallel to the wall are often too shallow to accommodate more than a few garments. The variable shapes of closets also suggest that period owners whose clothes were hung from pegs on the wall before the twentieth century did not demand more standardized spaces since they still used chests or wardrobes.

By the second half of the nineteenth century, manufactured clothing gave prosperous people access to larger collections of garments. Instead of having one suit of clothes, a middle-class man might have three or four; women could amplify their collections of dresses and have separate sets of garments for different occasions. Clothes closets would need to be modified or rethought to meet this new array of clothing that had to be stored when it was not being worn.

At the same time, industrialization gave rise to large disparities in wealth and in the size of dwellings and wardrobes, so there are class and regional differences in who has which kinds of clothes and closets. Some had no clothing to speak of, as Frederick Douglass recounts in his biographies. As a child of enslaved people, he was always cold because he only had rags to wear; on cold nights he crawled into a burlap bag in search of protection from the chilly night air.

Architectural pattern books give us a cross-section view of how clothes closets were conceived in the decades of industrialization. In William Ranlett's pattern book of 1849, he published designs for houses at diverse costs, from the simple parsonage to the grand villa. But even in his larger houses, clothes closets did not reliably appear. His Anglo-Grecian Villa with rooms arranged in four wings contained four bedrooms on the second floor, but only two of the four had clothes closets. In Andrew Jackson Downing's *Cottage Residences* in 1842, he mentioned the utility of closets and asserted that their usefulness was "universally acknowledged." Downing's 1850 *The Architecture of Country Houses* treated closets without much comment— they were simply taken to be normal. How many closets should be provided in a house appeared to depend on the class of the owner, and most of his farmhouse designs either had no clothes closets or very shallow ones on the bedroom level.

In E. C. Hussey's 1875 pattern book *Home Building*, a design for a farmhouse has five second-floor bedrooms, all without a clothes closet.[10] Farm families in the later nineteenth century often had very few resources. In an account written by a woman from a farm family in Minnesota, she described the family farmhouse: the only storage cupboard was one informally assembled from shipping boxes and grocery crates, which stood in the main room. The main room on the ground floor was their "kitchen, dining room, sitting room, and sometimes bedroom." The mother washed and ironed clothes, did all the cooking and baking, and sewed and mended here. Upstairs was an unfinished attic; there were no closets.[11]

A consistent closet size was not always demanded because some people substituted a wardrobe cabinet or press such as the one recommended by A. J. Downing in his 1850 book. This wardrobe had one compartment for hanging dresses and other full-length garments from pegs or hooks, and another compartment on the other side for a set of shelves on which folded

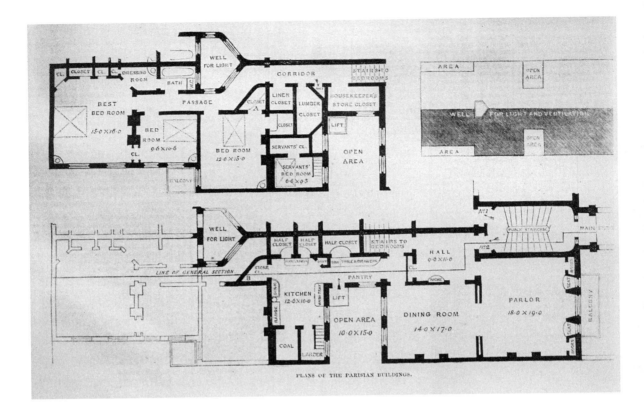

PLANS OF THE PARISIAN BUILDINGS.

garments could be stored.[12] Such wardrobe pieces supplemented the closet space afforded in houses, or replaced it in houses without closets. In the 1864 edition of his pattern book *Villas and Cottages*, Calvert Vaux offered a design for a lady's bedroom with two closets. His drawing shows the elevation of a bedroom wall with a center window framed by a projecting symmetrical pair of closets. This pattern of two projecting closets framing a niche remained popular into the twentieth century, the niche often housing a window seat or a dressing table.[13]

Catherine Beecher and Harriet Beecher Stowe presented a movable closet as a room divider in their 1869 *American Woman's Home*. As a strategy to make smaller, more economical houses work, they recommended dedicating one room for daytime use, and then converting that one room into two rooms at night by sliding the room divider into place. The wheeled room divider had pictures mounted on one side for display during the day, and when shifted to its position in the center of the room, it revealed outfitted storage on its other side with clothes hooks and shelves for various wardrobe items. Closets used as room dividers reappeared in the twentieth century as a strategy for creating two bedrooms out of one.

Fig. 86. Closets for specific users. Architect Calvert Vaux in the 1850s was one of the few early architects to design ample storage closets. In his split-level "Parisian Buildings" apartment design, he proposed a hall closet, a housekeepers' store closet, a lumber closet, a linen closet, seven bedroom closets distributed among three bedrooms, a servant's room closet, and three half-closets. *Harper's Weekly* 1 (December 19, 1857): 809.

 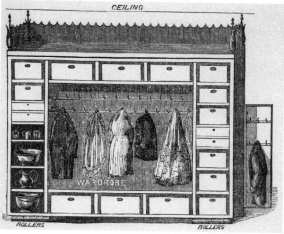

Fig. 87a and Fig. 87b. Beecher and Stowe's idea for a movable closet served as a room-divider to turn a daytime sitting room into two bedrooms at night. Their wheeled room divider had pictures mounted on one side for display during the day, but when shifted to its nighttime position in the center of the room, the divider/closet revealed an outfitted storage side with clothes hooks and shelves for various wardrobe items. Catherine E. Beecher and Harriet Beecher Stowe, *American Woman's Home* (1864; repr., New Brunswick: Rutgers Univ. Press, 2002).

Late nineteenth-century designers provided closets more reliably than those in the eighteenth century, and clothes closets proliferated across the span of middle- and upper-class houses. Clothes closets were principally supplied in bedrooms, although coat closets near the front door also became quite common in more expensive houses. Outfitting clothes closets with multiple drawers and shelves for specialized storage can be seen in the Beecher sisters' movable room divider-closet and in Mr. Glessner's 1880s Chicago dressing room. Nineteenth-century designers and builders continued to use very variable closet sizes.

In this era middle-class families could acquire a lot more possessions, which came on the market through industrial production. Some felt discomfort around having excessive material goods and feared that so many possessions would displace spiritual values. Architectural critic Henry Urbach wrote that nineteenth-century closets served to "moderate display without diminishing actual possession."[14] Closets allowed people, then as now, to acquire plentiful goods but keep them concealed.

As house plans developed in the twentieth century, clothes closets, increasingly widespread, began to receive further design attention. The magazine *Carpentry and Building* held competitions for economical house designs in the late nineteenth and early twentieth centuries. Competition entries from 1893 and 1902 show bedroom closets in nearly every bedroom, albeit in varied sizes and proportions.[15] The Radford Company sold house plans and specifications to mail-order customers from a selection published in their 1908 catalog, and the house #7067B offered adequate closets in each of the four bedrooms on the chamber floor. In the bungalow #5127 each of three bedrooms had a differently shaped closet; the odd shapes of federal period closets continued in lower-budget houses.

The general dimensions and proportions of a modern clothes closet are determined by how a hanger hangs from a closet bar. The clothes hangers of the type that we use now to hang clothes were developed over the course of the nineteenth century. Thomas Jefferson is said to have designed a wooden clothes hanger, and the Shakers were producing wood hangers at least by the 1850s to hang clothes from pegs around the walls of their rooms. An 1869 patent was awarded to O. A. North for a clothes hook shaped like a coat hanger. Common wire coat hangers were not invented until 1903 by A. J. Parkhouse, whose employer took out a patent on it in 1904.[16] Thus consistent clothes closet sizes based on standard clothes hangers could only develop in the twentieth century.

Small houses of the 1910s regularly made room for adequate closets that were fitted with bars for coat hangers. Dwellings produced for shipyard workers in 1918 Portsmouth provided regularized closet space with bars for hangers. The standard of bars for clothes hangers is evident in the book *Authentic Small Houses of the Twenties* with designs by the Architects' Small House Service Bureau.[17] All the two-bedroom bungalows have good-sized closets in the bedrooms. Although generally more adequately sized, clothes

Fig. 88. Closets fitted for storing specific items. Lydia Ray Balderston's 1928 economical house design called for a fitted closet with special shoe storage. Other closets mentioned in 1920s and 1930s magazine articles called for closets fitted for gun storage for men and sports equipment for boys. *Housewifery*, 5th ed. (J.B. Lippincott, 1936), 229.

closets in this era are still sometimes awkwardly deep or have inaccessible corners, but no house lacks closets in any bedroom. In several houses, though not all, the closets are paired and located between two bedrooms, which provides soundproofing between the rooms while meeting storage needs.

In the 1930s and 1940s, shelter magazines published numerous articles on decorating closets. They promoted wallpapers and borders, carpet, storage boxes with matching trim, function-specific racks, shelves, and containers, and mirrors to enhance closet interiors. Making the most of the closets in one's house meant hanging the bar or rail to maximize space above and below hanging clothes, using the wasted top and bottom spaces for shoes, hats, and other items. Closets gave a methodical or systematic way to organize people's possessions rather than just piling them all together in a trunk.[18]

Magazine articles recommended many specialized gadgets in the 1940s since they felt that middle-class people had amassed more clothes than the average house's closets could handle. Some of these were flexible hat stands that you could bend down to retrieve the hat or storage boxes with windowed fronts and sides, which came in colors and chintz or paper patterns to "tie in with your closet's color scheme." Specialized hangers included padded hangers covered in quilted satin, plastic ones in many colors, a ring-shaped hanger for a fur scarf or sweater, pole hangers that hung from the ceiling to raise a long garment up out of the way, and hangers with curved-up ends to keep evening gowns from slipping off.[19]

In the 1940s gender differences were supported in closet allocation and modification. A modern house in Connecticut published in *House and Garden* had one closet for the husband and three closets for the wife; her dressing table claimed space against a wall between two of them.[20] A *House Beautiful* article promoted individualized closets for different family members. The father's closet had a locked cabinet for rifles and cupboards for fishing rods, tackle, and ammunition.[21] A closet for a boy had more boxes, shelves, and cupboards to hold sporting equipment; since he stored fewer clothes, he may not have even needed a hanging bar. It is characteristic of post–World War II houses that the clothes closets and dressing rooms are allotted increasingly large amounts of square footage.

In the 1970s and 1980s architects working with diverse budgets added generous extra clothes storage in the form of walk-in closets and dressing rooms for both elite and middling clients. High-rent city apartment residents were likely to be childless professional couples who spent much of their time outside the dwelling. Entertaining was typically done in restaurants, so large living rooms and dining rooms could be omitted from the dwelling. Instead, the square footage was poured into spaces dedicated to bodily care. His and hers walk-in closets and dressing rooms accommodated a larger investment in clothing and a certain narcissistic interest in admiring oneself in mirrors. Some contemporary realtors assert that a house is worth less if its storage space comprises less than 20 percent of its square footage.[22]

For A. J. Downing in 1850, closets were tokens in a space game: he says about a cottage, "The first floor might be improved by turning the bedroom into a parlor. In this case the two closets . . . may be dispensed with" and their square footage redistributed to make the ground floor "much more spacious and agreeable." Similarly he describes a closet in the kitchen of the same cottage. If this closet were entirely thrown to the kitchen "it would make a good storeroom," but if desired, half this closet could be opened to the adjacent bedroom where it would make a second clothes closet. Downing was thinking of how he could shift functions while keeping the same square footage in this house, and in the planning stage closet space is shiftable.[23]

Architecturally, we can think of clothes closets as changing in formal type as they meet specific thresholds of improvement. If the starting point is a house without any clothes closets, for example, then the first threshold would be to build a closet—a defined space instead of an ad hoc or adapted space for clothing storage. To have a closet implies that you have articles of clothing in such numbers that they need to be stored and that you want to store your clothing in a concealed way. At this simple level most of the square footage of the house's interior is visible space, a very small percentage being used for hidden closet space. The next threshold of improvement would be having closets of regular shapes matched to their purpose of clothes storage on hangers, followed by providing a closet big enough to enter—walk-in closets or dressing rooms comprise this larger type and became common for middle-class suburban houses in the 1970s. At this point the closet has become a room, with enough square footage to make it nearly comparable to others in the house. The next threshold might be a closet big enough to walk into that has a window for light—it might even become a place where friends are invited to observe one's apparel collection. This clothes closet has become what the very first closet was—a small private room—now not for study but for containing material goods.

Clothes closets also belong in the category of identity producers in a house—along with street facades, front lawns, and cars—that tell viewers who you are and what your status is. The street façade of a house informs passersby about your household's taste and financial standing, while the clothes in your closet testify to the same for you as an individual. One gets dressed in the selection of clothing designed to present one's identity to the public, an identity that may change for specific occasions. Sociologist Saulo Cwerner writes, "The bedroom has become, at least in more affluent societies, the refuge of the personal self, and clothing has been instrumental in fashioning this personality." So the wardrobe is the space of individuality and it contains a person's biography in the form of clothing. Modern people have a variety of identities and occupy different roles as they belong to various social or cultural groups, and these different identities can be mobilized by a visit to the clothes closet.[24] In a 1996 article, Henry Urbach describes the closet as a site of storage that is connected to spaces of display yet that is not for display itself: a bedroom needs the closet even while it renders invisible its space and its contents.[25]

Storage Outside the House

Many householders do not have large enough dwellings to provide adequate storage space for tools, toys, and seasonal equipment. Apartments tend to have no extra storage in the dwelling unit except for typical closets, though there may be a storage unit in the building basement for each household. People end up doing their best to store out-of-season goods, toys, and clothing passed down from older siblings, strollers and bicycles and what have you, but they often enlist spaces not intended for storage. Many turn to rental storage units away from the homescape.

Fig. 89. Outdoor storage. Balconies, porches, and backyards become storage locations when indoor spaces and containers fall short. Outdoor spaces, such as this backyard at Galesville, Virginia, are commonly used for out-of-season storage like barbecue grills or bicycles, picnic tables or air-conditioners. Photo E. C. Cromley.

One convenient place for storing things at the house is a balcony or porch. Such an outdoor appendage could be a nice luxury, a place to sit in pleasant weather, but without anywhere else to store things, many balconies become storage closets. Seasonal furniture, sports equipment, laundry carts, off-season bikes, or extra mops and buckets find a home on the balcony. Others have appropriated parts of the yard to store tangentially useful items that won't fit inside a garage, shed, or cellar. In a Joy Williams short story, the narrator tells us, "All the stuff that got broke was put in the front yard under the tarp. . . . It wasn't garbage under there, it was just stuff that got broke and where was that supposed to go?"[26] Many a yard in rural America has a no-longer-working refrigerator or an old car waiting in the yard for a new use or a repair, or just to rust away.

A garage is another outdoor space designed for storage. Positioned behind or beside the house, the first garages were freestanding buildings. At elite houses, garages accommodated car repair equipment, turntables orienting the car forward when someone was ready to drive it away, or even an apartment for the chauffeur who both drove the car and maintained it. Smaller garages for middling houses were fitted to the size of the cars that would be stored in them. The size of a garage was typically indicated in its name: a one-car or a two-car garage (similar to the way house sizes are indicated today by naming the number of bedrooms).

However, for the later twentieth century the proliferation of goods has required of the garage an adaptability to store household excess. Because the garage is outside the house proper, it can accommodate dirt, so garden-

Fig. 90. Attached garages in suburban and rural settings are typically used for additional storage. Not only cars, for which garages were designed, but also gardening tools, ladders, sports equipment, and all sorts of other items get stored there. Levitt developers, c. 1961 Belair subdivision at Bowie, MD. Photo E. C. Cromley.

ing tools and equipment often find a home in the garage. Likewise, carpentry and home-repair tools can be found in garages where their sharp or rough character will not disturb indoor space. Sporting goods may be best stored there, especially objects that are larger than closets in the house can handle—bicycles, nets and racquets, bats and mitts. And is there still room to store the car?

There are several ways to conceptualize storage spaces in and near houses—purpose-built storage spaces such as root cellars, pantries, garages, and clothes closets; ad hoc appropriated storage spaces such as balconies, cellars, and attics; and elements of the landscape such as backyards that are asked to serve as informal storage. The amount of material being stored depends on the level of income and the lifestyle of inhabitants—prosperous households own more goods and need more space to store it in than occupants of poor households, while families living in houses with children probably have more goods to store than single occupants of studio apartments. Storage is often required seasonally yet differs by region, so bathing suits and baseball equipment in New England will be stored in winter, while the same items in Florida may never need storing.

When considered as architectural space, cabinets and closets represent the trade-offs in square footage between hidden and visible lives in houses. The simple, one-room cabin or worker's cottage throws all its square footage into visible space, where a reused packing crate in the room might be the only storage unit. Elite houses in the Federal period typically had clothes closets in only some of the bedrooms, and often these had odd shapes that resulted from the non-rectilinear rooms leaving leftover spaces behind their walls. Well-to-do householders displayed their finest dining items in purpose-built china closets, while home economists developed kitchens that contained pots and pans, dishes, and glassware in specialized cabinetry. The increasing size of built-for-the-purpose cabinets and closets shows not a smooth growth curve but sporadic changes, as designers calculated how much storage would make suitable houses for the various classes. Modern dwellings at every class level now have closets included, but the greater amount of square footage given to closet space distinguishes expensive dwellings.

7

CONCLUSION

The preceding chapters give examples of people using houses as they engaged in the common activities of cooking, socializing, eating, sleeping, moving around the house, and storing their goods. When we step back for an overview, some themes emerge that cut across these activities. How does the specialization of spaces operate over time and how shall we value it? Do the types of household labor available at any particular time effect the form of rooms? Do manners—formal or informal—help shape the use of spaces? How are private versus public boundaries manifested in the architecture of houses? Does the desire for convenience lead to steady improvements in house arrangements? As you visit houses and think about how they work, you will ask many more questions of your own.

How does specialization of spaces operate over time? The arc of development seems to go from the early house in which one room served all purposes, to a nineteenth-century house that had a specialized room for each household activity. Cooking space evolved from a large fireplace and its tools at one end of the one- or two-room house, to an addition at the back of the house for a new cooking fireplace in a lean-to or a cast-iron cookstove in a kitchen ell. By the early twentieth century, gas or electric-powered ranges combined with plumbed sinks and electric refrigerators in a kitchen dedicated to food storage and preparation and pared of other uses.

Likewise in an arc of specialization for sleeping space, people initially slept wherever they found a place to lie down in rustic cabins and attics. The first step in specializing a sleeping space occurred when the owners in a household placed a well-furnished bedstead in their parlor or chamber and enjoyed a little privacy as well as the admiration of visitors seeing their expensive bed. The specialization of sleeping spaces continued as more middling and upper-class households built several bedrooms per house and began to make guests', boys', and girls' rooms part of their aim to specialize.

Such specialization has continued into the present with bedrooms for each member of a household when owners can afford them.

Cutting down on the number of rooms with specialized purposes has somewhat reversed this arc in the twentieth century. Combining dining with living-room and family-room functions tends to make the combined spaces usable throughout the day and evening. It trades the specialized aspects that supported the dining function for the generalized usefulness of a merged space. Yet many express regret that the family never sits down to a meal together. Is there a loss to the family from giving up the architectural framework of proper meals? Kitchens were once paired with pantries where calibrated storage shelves, cupboards, and drawers made a spot for each piece of china, glassware, and equipment. In omitting pantries and their specialized storage and trading it for the generic storage of kitchen cabinets, steps were saved for the housewife, but the specialized pantry-type storage is now only available in very expensive kitchen renovations and new builds.

How does changing household labor affect rooms? Until the WWI era, extra labor commonly supplemented the home labor of the owners or housewife. Colonial-era owners at a broad range of incomes purchased the labor of apprentices, indentured servants, or enslaved workers to cook, launder, and clean; repair goods; and otherwise take on household tasks. Servants who lived in the house or on the grounds needed a room to stay in, although it was often a leftover space also used for storage. In nineteenth-century servant-run houses, women servants often occupied the attic while a male butler had an apartment in the basement, segregating the sexes. Nicely designed servants' bedrooms in the later nineteenth and early twentieth centuries, plus a servants' hall in wealthier households, placed a requirement for extra furnished rooms on middle- and upper-class house builders.

The introduction of piped water, electricity, gas, and central heating cut down on the need for servants to light fireplaces for heat, keep lamps and candles ready, or pump water. When job markets offered factory positions, servants found better jobs and turned away from household work for something more independent and better paying. They preferred to live in their own houses or apartments with their own families rather than in their employers' houses. Over the decades houses became smaller and more efficient, accommodating the shortage of labor while benefiting from the extra space released by the absence of servants' rooms from the family dwelling.

Women's agency in shaping space is another issue that cuts across our previous themes. Nineteenth-century mothers always wanted to keep an eye on their young children and asked builders to locate a nursery near the kitchen. Once the kitchen was not occupied by servants, housewives wanted to share in the activities of not just the nursery but all the other social rooms in the house, rethinking the relationship of their workspaces to the rest of the family's rooms. Open kitchens of the post-WWII era connected family members and guests with the housewife, inviting others into the kitchen where once just the maid labored.

How do manners help shape the use and furnishing of spaces? Consider the manners that apply to middle- and upper-middle-class social spaces in the mid-nineteenth century compared to those in the early twentieth century. The earlier era tried to segregate a purified social space from the rest of domestic activity by furnishing an impressive parlor. The parlor, only occupied by visitors who had arranged to call at a certain day and time, held the finest furniture and artistic ornaments. Both visitors and residents were expected to display their best manners, keep to specific conversational gambits, and wear the correct clothing for parlor visits. Parlors occupied the front of the house, often overlooking the street.

Later when parlors were replaced by living rooms, the informal manners of family conviviality applied; then social rooms aimed to make people comfortable, engaged them in recreational activities or small-scale handiwork, and encouraged interactions among all ages. Living rooms, like parlors, would be located at the front of the house, but furnished in plain, simple materials—smooth oak chairs instead of carved rosewood with velvet upholstery, for example. In both cases visitors would encounter the social room before seeing the rest of the interior, but upon being received into the social room, visitors would observe the prevailing manners and respond with controlled or relaxed behavior.

Similarly, the correct manners that surrounded dining would prescribe matching chairs, a dining table, a sideboard, and a china closet to provide suitable support for more formal meals. A prosperous family seated around its dining table would be served by a maid and begin eating at a signal from the hostess. As informal manners took over at the turn of the twentieth century, dining in a well-appointed dining room began to seem stuffy, and—only used a couple of hours a day—as wasted space. Householders incorporated easily moved tables, benches, and chairs into the ends of living rooms and kitchens to eat on. They built kitchen counters that extended out to receive stools where family members could perch for informal meals. The old dining room, now only a site for dinners a few times a year on holidays and family occasions, became a kind of general-purpose room for doing school homework, making model airplanes, or solving puzzles. Postwar developers of low-cost houses stopped building dining rooms in new houses to save buyers money. At the expensive end of development, buyers wanted combined family-living-dining kitchens to meet the informal manners of the late twentieth century.

In eras where manners are formal for the middle and upper classes there tend to be prescribed practices and rules for people's interactions. Such rules are designed to maintain the social rank of participants, distinguishing between elites and those perceived to be of lower status. In that era, separate staircases for owners and servants kept the classes from mixing but doubled some of the circulation paths. In eras where more informal manners prevail, everyone is perceived as more or less equal and even children are granted a place. Now we need not segregate anyone to a separate staircase.

Private versus public boundaries can be manifested in the architecture of houses. The simplest acknowledgement of this difference is the front door. Householders have always organized their living spaces with an eye to who lives there and who comes from outside. When one enters an early house, the door may convey a defensive aspect, protecting the interior, declaring everyone outside the door to be the public and everyone within to constitute the private family. Yet once you enter there may be no barrier between a visitor and the rest of the one-room abode; public flows freely into private.

As houses develop more rooms in subsequent decades, filters between public space outside and private space within become more sophisticated. Perhaps the family had built a small vestibule; then when you enter you aren't yet inside personal space. Whoever receives visitors will direct you further into the family rooms or perhaps ask you to wait in the vestibule, or even to leave. More vestibules, halls, passages, and doors create stages of moving from public to private.

Within larger houses of the eighteenth and nineteenth centuries interior rooms were also identified as more public or more private. Main-floor social rooms—typically the parlor and dining room—received visitors and thus had a more public nature. Sometimes a home office on the same floor received business visitors, also in the category of the public. Second-floor rooms tended to belong to the private sphere; closest friends and family members would penetrate to the second floor and feel comfortable in these rooms. Within the private zone of the house there are also gradations of publicity-to-privacy. Halls, corridors, and stairs are the more public elements; individual bedrooms or bathrooms are the private spaces.

Levels of architectural ornament often point to which spaces are public and which private. The more public spaces are typically enriched with moldings, carvings, columns, wallpapers, and other embellishments. Service rooms were private to the servants, the owners who managed them, and delivery men or messengers. Private spaces have lighter enrichment and service spaces are left without much or any ornament. Manners must be combined with architectural signals to urge that everyone observes these boundaries.

We all desire convenience in our houses, but has it led to steady improvements in house arrangements? In some areas, houses have become more and more convenient. Indoor plumbing, for example, delivers hot and cold water to bathrooms, kitchens, and sometimes the basement, the summer kitchen, and other recreation rooms. Hot water may also deliver heat to all the rooms in a steam or hot-water heating system. The supply of water, accessible just where it is used, is surely an improvement in convenience over going to the backyard pump. Few would assert that using a well-kept, modern indoor bathroom is less convenient than using an outdoor privy.

In room distribution and enclosure, however, some dwellers object that having modern open plans cuts down on convenience. The formerly enclosed living room, dining room, family room, and kitchen are now open to each other. When adults want to have quiet conversations, the children are making noise in the family room. Open plans improve the social interactions of kitchen workers, but when the cooks have upended the usual order in the kitchen, do they want their dinner guests to see the mess? For some, convenience is enhanced by returning to more enclosed rooms.

The convenience of storage facilities built into modern houses is valuable. Our kitchen cabinets make for sleek and orderly kitchens, our bedroom closets for safely stored wardrobes. But has anyone been in the attic lately? A couple who packed up their belongings to move to another city finally checked the basement for stored items. Six dump trucks of stuff were hauled out. Our consumption patterns leave us with objects that have passed from use but still remain in storage in capacious houses.

Many of the ambitions for improving how houses work over the centuries have led to both positive and negative outcomes. We like privacy but we do not like to be excluded. We hope for more convenient houses with automated light, heat, and cooling, but that leads us to digital service systems that sell our personal data. We enjoy the light and air of our houses' open planning, yet we sometimes miss the containment of specific domestic activities in rooms of their own. We just have to keep on trying.

NOTES

INTRODUCTION

1. I have been researching and writing about American dwellings for many years, so readers who know my previous work will find some familiar examples and arguments repeated here. E. C. Cromley's publications that bear on this book's content: *The Food Axis: Cooking, Eating, and the Architecture of American Houses* (Charlottesville: Univ. of Virginia Press, 2010); co-author with Thomas Carter, *Invitation to Vernacular Architecture* (Knoxville: Univ. of Tennessee Press, 2000); *Alone Together: A History of New York's Early Apartments* (Ithaca: Cornell Univ. Press, 1990); "Masculine/Indian," *Winterthur Portfolio* (Spring 1997); "Transforming the Food Axis: Houses, Tools, Modes of Analysis," *Material History Review* (Ottawa, National Museum of Science, Fall 1996); "Aspects of the History of the American Bedroom," *Perspectives in Vernacular Architecture* 4 (Univ. of Missouri Press, 1991): 177–86; "Modernizing—or 'You never see a screen door on affluent homes,'" *Journal of American Culture* 5 (Summer 1982): 71–79.

2. Style may affect the functionality of houses in that houses using classical symmetry tend to have squared-off rooms and symmetrical plans while houses in a romantic style have more bay windows, porches, and irregular profiles. One book that explains the features of American architectural style is Virginia and Lee McAlester, *A Field Guide to American Houses* (New York: Alfred Knopf, 2000). Others are listed in the bibliography.

3. Architect Christopher Alexander urges architects to design buildings that will encourage and support extra activities in undefined small spaces at the edges of an otherwise familiar room type. See Alexander and Sara Ishikawa, Murray Silverstein, with Max Jacobson, Ingrid Fiksdahl-King, Shlomo Angel, *A Pattern Language: Towns, Buildings, Construction* (New York: Oxford Univ. Press, 1977). Renee Chow's book *Suburban Space: The Fabric of Dwelling* (Berkeley: Univ. of California Press, 2002) explores the furnishing patterns developed by renters to make their apartment rooms match their needs, regardless of the designer's original intentions for the room.

1. SPACES FOR COOKING

1. Ellen Plante, *The American Kitchen, 1700 to the Present* (New York: Facts on File, 1995); Priscilla J. Brewer, From Fireplace to Cookstove, *Technology and the Domestic Ideal in America* (Syracuse: Syracuse Univ. Press, 2000). Many of these ideas first published in Cromley, *Food Axis*.

2. Abbott Cummings, *Framed Houses of Massachusetts Bay* (Cambridge: Harvard Univ. Press, 1979): 29–30; inventories show that sometimes anomalous goods were stored in service rooms, such as the scales and weights and linen yarn stored in Michael Bacon's Dedham buttery, 1649 inventory, p. 29; Cummings, "Three Hearths," *Old Time New England* (Spring 1997): 21.

3. Fraser D. Neiman, "Domestic Architecture at the Clifts Plantation: the Social Context of Early Virginia Building," in *Common Places—Readings in American Vernacular Architecture*, eds. D. Upton and J. M. Vlach (Athens and London: Univ. of Georgia Press, 1986).

4. Fraser D. Neiman, "Domestic Architecture at the Clifts," 310.

5. Robert Beverley, *The History and Present State of Virginia*, with an Introduction by Louis B. Wright (Chapel Hill: Univ. of North Carolina Press, 1947), 290.

6. Abbott Cummings, "Three Hearths," *Old-Time New England* (Spring 1997): 25.

7. Kenneth R. LeVan, *Building Construction and Materials of the Pennsylvania Germans* (Harrisburg, VAF, 2004): 46. In the Ephrata Cloister, an eighteenth-century utopian religious community in Pennsylvania, raised cooking hearths may be seen in the restored Saal or meeting hall.

8. Bernard Herman, *Town House, Architecture and Material Life in the Early American City, 1780–1830* (Chapel Hill: Univ. of North Carolina Press, 2005).

9. Whitney Battle, "A Space of our Own," in *Household Chores and Household Choices—Theorizing the Domestic Sphere in Historical Archaeology*, eds. Kerri Barile and Jamie Brandon (Tuscaloosa: Univ. of Alabama Press, 2004), 35–36.

10. Ste. Genevieve, Missouri, explored in the Vernacular Architecture Forum Annual Meeting guidebook, 1989, 98ff; see HABS drawings of the Bolduc House. George R. Brooks, "The Bolduc House in Ste. Genevieve, MO," Antiques 92 (July 1967): 96–97 gives the construction date at 1785.

11. George R. Brooks, "The Bolduc House" reproduces HABS drawings.

12. Julie Riesenweber and Karen Hudson, eds., *The Kentucky Bluegrass* (Vernacular Architecture Forum guidebook, 1990): 81–85.

13. T. Hubka, *Big House, Little House, Back House, Barn: The Connected Farm Buildings of New England* (Hanover, NH: Univ. Press of New England, 1984), 170.

14. Ritchie Garrison, *Landscape and Material Life in Franklin County, Massachusetts, 1770–1860* (Knoxville: Univ. of Tennessee Press, 1991), 163.

15. Garrison, Landscape, 168–72.

16. Marla R. Miller, "Labor and Liberty in an Age of Refinement," in *Building Environments—Perspectives in Vernacular Architecture* 10, eds. Breisch and Hoagland (Knoxville: Univ. of Tennessee Press, 2005), 17–19.

17. Richard M. Candee, *Building Portsmouth: The Neighborhoods and Architecture of New Hampshire's Oldest City* (Portsmouth: Portsmouth Advocates, 1992), 70, 72–73.

18. Richard M. Candee, *Building Portsmouth* details water supply in Portsmouth.

19. Ruth Schwartz Cowan, "The Consumption Junction: A Proposal for Research Strategies in the Sociology of Technology," in *The Social Construction of Technological Systems*, eds. Bijker, Hughes, and Pinch (Cambridge: MIT, 1987), 72–73.

20. Farnsworth Homestead brochure, n.d.

21. Lynne J. Belluscio, "Brick Ovens in the Genesee Country, 1789–1860: Architectural and Documentary Evidence," in *Foodways*, ed. Benes (New Hampshire: Dublin Seminar, 1982).

22. See Betsy Klimasmith, *At Home in the City: Urban Domesticity in American Literature and Culture, 1850–1930* (Durham: Univ. of New Hampshire Press, 2005), 90–127, chapter on tenements and Jacob Riis.

23. Alfred Kazin, *A Walker in the City* (New York: Grove Press, 1951), 53, 55.

24. Kazin, *Walker*, 65.

25. Catherine E. Beecher, *Treatise on Domestic Economy* (New York: Harper and Brothers, 1845). Catherine E. Beecher and Harriet Beecher Stowe, *American Woman's Home* (Hartford, CT: Harriet Beecher Stowe Center, 1864; repr. New Brunswick, NJ: Rutgers Univ. Press, 2002).

26. Frank T. Lent, architect, *Sound Sense in Suburban Architecture* (Cranford, NJ: self-published, 1893), 34–35; pantry as valve, see Ellen Lupton and Abbott Miller, *Kitchens, Bathrooms, and the Aesthetics of Waste* (Cambridge, MA: MIT List Visual Arts Center, 1992).

27. Melinda Haynes, *Mother of Pearl* (New York: Washington Square Press, 1999), 8 –9.

28. Lydia Ray Balderston, *Housewifery* (Philadelphia: Lippincott, 1919); this popular book was reprinted in 1921, 1924, 1928, and 1936.

29. E. Kohl, *Land of the Burnt Thigh, A Lively Story of Women Home-steaders on the South Dakota Frontier* (St. Paul: Minnesota Historical Society Press, 1986; first published 1938 by Funk and Wagnalls); Introduction by Glenda Riley, xiii–xiv, 2, 4, 13 (drawing of their shack with two people, p. 16).

30. E. Kohl, *Land of the Burnt Thigh*, xvii.

31. Kohl, *Land of the Burnt Thigh*, 94–95.

32. Kohl, *Land of the Burnt Thigh*, 135.

33. Fred W. Peterson, *Homes in the Heartland, Balloon Frame Farm-houses of the Upper Midwest, 1850–1920* (Lawrence: Univ. Press of Kansas, 1992), 54.

34. Peterson, *Homes in the Heartland*, 53–54

35. Carla Bianca, *The Two Rosetos* (Bloomington: Indiana Univ. Press, 1974), 24. A lot of socializing took place on the street, as it had back in their Italian homeland, where in good weather residents would carry tables and chairs to the sidewalk and engage in conversation.

36. Clara H. Zillessen, "Electricity in the Home. Household Refrigeration Without Ice," *House Beautiful* (April 1920): 318; David Nye, *Consuming Power: a Social History of American Energies* (Cambridge: MIT Press, 1998).

37. Richard Plunz, *A History of Housing In New York City* (New York: Columbia Univ. Press, 1990), 276; Barbara M. Kelly, *Expanding the American Dream—Building and Rebuilding Levittown* (Albany: SUNY Press, 1993); the first Levittown Cape Cod house, built as a rental dwelling, had two bedrooms—a reduction of the three-bedroom houses, which had dining rooms, that Levitt had been building before the war (65).

38. Jim Naughton, "Bigger is Better," *The Washington Post*, March 17, 2002.

39. Ibid.

40. Food Channel, Dec. 30, 2003.

41. Hongyan Yang, typescript, 2015, p. 10. A Madison, Wisconsin, house built for the Reisner family in 1909 currently hosts an immigrant Hmong family of five. On their attitude to storage of seasonings: "Everyone in the family, we taste when we cook, and keep tasting it until it tastes good. We

do that a lot, so it's more convenient to leave all the spices within reach and not put away."

42. Stephen Fan, ed., *Suburbanisms—Casino Urbanization, Chinatowns, and the Contested American Landscape* (New London, CT: Lyman Art Museum, 2014), 81, 121.

2. SOCIALIZING

1. The terms "great room" and "family room" have been in occasional use earlier; e.g., in Bruère, *The House That Jill Built After Jack's Had Proved a Failure* (New York: E. C. Gardner, 1882), the house plan on p. 239 features a family room instead of a parlor near the front entrance; Eberlein, article in *Architectural Record* 36 (Nov. 1914): 407 illustrates the "Great room" in the house of W. S. and J. T. Spaulding at Pride's Crossing, Massachusetts by architects Little and Browne. Family rooms are explored in James Jacobs, "Social and Spatial Change in the Postwar Family Room," *Buildings and Landscapes* 19, no. 1 (Spring 2012): 70–85.

2. House for the Hispanic governor of Texas in "The DeLeon-Massenet Expedition," in *Spanish Explorations in the Southwest, 1542–1750*, ed. Herbert Bolton (repr. Barnes and Noble, 1963).

3. See very-low-budget shelter-seekers in twenty-first-century Los Angeles: Jake Wegmann, "The Hidden Cityscapes of Informal Housing in Suburban Los Angeles," *Buildings and Landscapes* 22 (Fall 2015): 89–110; especially 100–101.

4. The "tiny house" movement of the 2010s has a television show as well as books promoting houses of one hundred to four hundred square feet.

5. Beth Twiss-Garrity, "Getting Comfortable" (MA thesis, Univ. of Delaware), 23. Best beds disappear from parlors at varying dates by region: in Wilmington, between 1780 and 1820 beds disappear from parlors. In New England Cummings says they are gone by the Revolution. She thinks that 1780–1820 was an era concerned with identifying the pieces of furniture in each room because room identity was in flux at that time. Earlier lists grouped everything together in a house and showed less concern for differentiating rooms; later, room names made contents obvious and general lists of furniture didn't need to be room by room.

6. Katherine C. Grier, *Culture and Comfort, People, Parlors and Upholstery* (Rochester, NY: The Strong Museum, 1988).

7. "A Parlor View in a New York Dwelling House," *Gleason's Pictorial Drawing Room Companion* (Nov. 11, 1854): 300. For photos of parlors,

see William Seale, *The Tasteful Interlude: American Interiors through the Camera's Eye, 1860–1917*, 2d ed. (Nashville, Tennessee: American Association for State and Local History, 1981).

8. James J. Farrell, *Inventing the American Way of Death* (Philadelphia: Temple Univ. Press, 1980), 175.

9. Dell Upton, "Pattern Books and Professionalism," *Winterthur Portfolio* 19 (Autumn 1984): 107–50.

10. E. C. Hussey, *Home Building . . . from New York to San Francisco* (New York: 1875), plate 27.

11. Charles Lakey's 1875 pattern book, *Village and Country Houses*.

12. For a survey of Chicago architectural work, see *Inland Architect*.

13. Glessner diary, February 11, 1888.

14. Edward Lee Young, "Remodeling the Commonplace Home—Part 3, The Library," *Decorator and Furnisher* 28 (April 1896): 6–7.

15. Katherine C. Grier, *Culture and Comfort: People, Parlors and Upholstery* (Rochester, NY: The Strong Museum, 1988).

16. Lakey, *Village*, 1875; "Cheap Houses for Mechanics," designs 45 and 46, plate 59.

17. Cromley, *Alone Together: A History of New York's Early Apartments* (Ithaca and London: Cornell Univ. Press, 1990), 84.

18. Bruère, *The House That Jill Built After Jack's Had Proved a Failure* (New York: E. C. Gardner, 1882), 509–10.

19. Mary Gay Humphreys, "House Decoration and Furnishing," in *The House and Home—a Practical Book II*, ed. Lyman Abbott et al. (New York: Charles Scribner's Sons, 1896), 103, 105.

20. Ethel Carpenter, *Ladies Home Journal* 39 (1922): 177–78.

21. "40 Houses," *Architectural Forum* 88 (April 1948): 93–144.

22. Sandy Isenstadt, *The Modern American House—Spaciousness and Middle Class Identity* (Cambridge and New York: Cambridge Univ. Press, 2006).

23. "40 Houses," *Architectural Forum* 88, 93–144 passim.

24. James Jacobs, "Social and Spatial Change in the Postwar Family Room," *Perspectives in Vernacular Architecture* 13, no. 1 (2006): 70–85.

25. Barbara Miller Lane, *Houses for a New World* (Princeton: Princeton Univ. Press, 2016), 241.

26. Memories of kitchens used as living rooms reported by realtor Linda Morelli in conversation with the author, 2002, and design historian Regina Blasczyk, in conversation, 1999.

27. Ann Hood, "Memories of My Mother's Kitchen," *Bon Appetit*, Nov. 1999, 60–62.

28. O. S. Fowler, *The Octagon House* (New York: 1853; repr. Dover, 1973).

29. For discussion of taking down walls and opening up kitchens, see Cromley, *The Food Axis*, 207–18.

30. "Living-Kitchen," *Architectural Forum* 82 (May 1945): 107–12.

31. Ruth Cowan, *More Work for Mother: The Ironies of Household Technology from the Open Hearth to the Microwave* (New York: Basic, 1983).

32. Kenmore advertisement in *Bon Appetit*, Sept. 1999, 9–11.

33. Jan Gleysteen and Brad Walker, "Clarke/Freeze" presentation at Boston Cyclorama, Feb. 9, 2006.

34. Fred Bernstein, "Are McMansions Going Out of Style?" *New York Times*, Oct. 2, 2005, citing the US Census Bureau statistics. Peter Andrew, "Is your house the 'Typical American Home' in 2019?" HSH.com, July 28, 2019.

35. "Pure Vermont," *Metropolitan Home* 27 (July–Aug. 1995): 69–71.

36. Julie V. Iovine, "Designers Arrive in the Kitchen with Creature Comforts," *New York Times*, July 9, 1998.

37. Deborah Baldwin, "Why So Cold, My Proud Beauty?" *New York Times*, Dec. 16, 2004.

38. delete note [AU/UTP: Add content for this note. Location in main text: page 49, second paragraph, first sentence.]

3. SPACES FOR EATING

1. James E. McWilliams, *A Revolution in Eating* (New York: Columbia Univ. Press, 2005). Ideas in this chapter first developed in Cromley, *Food Axis*.

2. Ann Yentsch, "Expressions of Cultural Variation," 127–28.

3. Mary Beaudry et al., "A Vessel Typology for Early Chesapeake Ceramics—The Potomac Typological System," in *Documentary Archaeology*, ed. Beaudry (Cambridge: Cambridge Univ. Press, 1988), 55.

4. *Journal of Jasper Danckaerts* (Dec. 1679; repr. New York: Barnes and Noble, 1913), 148.

5. Heal, *The Language and Symbolism of Hospitality*, 3, quoted George Wheler's 1698 definition of hospitality: "a Liberal Entertainment of all sorts of Men, at one's House, whether Neighbors or Strangers, with Kindness, especially with Meat, Drink, and Lodgings."

6. Cummings, *Framed Houses*, 39.

7. Cummings, "Three Hearths," 39.

8. Camille Wells, "Virginia By Design: The Making of Tuckahoe And The Remaking Of Monticello," *Arris: Journal Of The Southeast Chapter Of The Society Of Architectural Historians* 12 (2001): 44–73. Mark Wenger, "The Dining Room in Early Virginia," in *Perspectives in Vernacular Architecture* 3, eds. Herman and Carter (Columbia: Univ. of Missouri Press, 1990), 149–59; Richard Bushman, *The Refinement of America: Persons, Houses, Cities* (New York: Knopf, 1992).

9. Mark Wenger, "The Dining Room in Early Virginia," in *Perspectives in Vernacular Architecture* 3, eds. Herman and Carter, 149–59.

10. Dell Upton, "Vernacular Domestic Architecture in Eighteenth-Century Virginia," in *Common Places—Readings in American Vernacular Architecture*, eds. D. Upton and J. M. Vlach (Athens and London: Univ. of Georgia Press, 1986), 315–35; 321.

11. The expense of candles for lighting is discussed in Jane Brox, *Brilliant: the Evolution of Artificial Light* (Boston and New York: Houghton Mifflin Harcourt, 2010), 12–15.

12. Bernard L. Herman, *Town House: Architecture and Material Life in the Early American City, 1780–1830* (Chapel Hill: Univ. of North Carolina Press, 2005), 193, 195.

13. *Observations sur les Moeurs de las Habitans de la Nouvelle Angleterre, 1797* (Winterthur Museum and Library, Manuscript Collection), 34.

14. An example is the c. 1830 Old Merchant's House in Greenwich Village, New York; even elite householders might put dining rooms in the basement, as seen at the 1860–61 Bellamy Mansion in Wilmington, North Carolina.

15. See Kenneth Ames, "Death in the Dining Room," in his collection of essays *Death in the Dining Room and Other Tales of Victorian Culture* (Philadelphia: Temple Univ. Press, 1992), 44–96. Deer-head lamps illustrated in *Old House Interiors* 1 (Winter 1995): 24.

16. In contrast to nature themes, in Mary Northend's photograph of the Tucker family's dining room, the walls themselves are almost covered by a collection of plates and platters, while additional platters are displayed on the mantelpiece and on shelves surrounding the mirror above the fireplace. Using china to ornament a dining room reaches back to the eighteenth century, when ornamental cupboards displaying china were built into the corners of rooms used for dining

17. John F. Kasson, "Rituals of Dining: Table Manners in Victorian America," in *Dining in America 1850–1900*, ed. Kathryn Grover (Amherst:

Univ. of Massachusetts Press, 1987), 135, quoting Timothy Edward Howard, *Excelsior; or Essays on Politeness, Education, and the Means of Attaining Success in Life* (1868).

18. Fortescue Cuming, *Sketches of a Tour to the Western Country . . . in the Winter of 1807 and concluded in 1809* (Pittsburgh: Cramer, Spear, and Eichenbaum, 1810), 41. "Mr. Ramsey with a stranger [Mr. Cuming], seated himself to dinner, while his wife in the patriarchal mode, very common in this country, attended table." The Ramseys' house also had a second room in which there were two beds and a hand loom where most of the family's clothes were woven. In the cellar were two or three tubs of lard and a "lump of tobacco."

19. Rebecca Burlend, *A True Picture of Emigration or Fourteen Years in the Interior of North America* (London: G. Berger, 1848), 21.

20. Booker T. Washington, *Up from Slavery* (Oxford and New York: Oxford Univ. Press, 1995).

21. "Built-in furniture," *House and Garden* 23 (March 1913): 197.

22. Ibid.

23. Edward W. Bok, "Abolish the Dining Room," *Collier's: The National Weekly* (Jan. 15, 1927): 10.

24. Ibid. Of course there was no formal dining room in American houses until the eighteenth century for the wealthy and the mid-nineteenth for the middle class.

25. "The Dining Room as a Center of Hospitality and Good Cheer," *The Craftsman* 9 (Nov. 1905): 229–36.

26. *Houses by Mail*, 96.

27. William Radford, *Architectural Details for Every Type of Building* (Chicago: Radford Architecture Co., 1921; repr. Dover, 2002): 38.

28. Rick Marin, "Closed by Order of the Cook," Guy Décor column, *New York Times*, June 15, 2006.

29. "A Small House with 'Lots of Room in It,'" *Ladies' Home Journal* (1901), in *Frank Lloyd Wright, Collected Writings*, 76.

30. Elizabeth Sweeney Herbert, "This is How I Keep House," *McCall's* (April 1949) 41–44, quoted in Kelly, *Levittown*, 66. McCall's called Mrs. Eckhoff's kitchen "this convenient kitchen-laundry-dining room."

31. Barbara Miller Lane, *Houses for a New World: Builders and Buyers in the American Suburbs, 1945–1965* (Princeton: Princeton Univ. Press, 2015), 242.

32. Kelly, *Levittown*, 83–84.

33. Richard Plunz, *A History of Housing In New York City* (New York: Columbia Univ. Press, 1990), 256; the architects for the East River houses were Voorhees, Walker, Foley, Smith, Alfred Easton Poor, and C. W. Schlusing, 244–45.

34. Lane, *Houses for a New World*, 239.

35. Otto Teegan, "Houses in Our Towns of Tomorrow," in *The Arts and Decoration Book of Successful Houses* (New York: McBride, 1940), 91–92.

36. Royal Barry Wills, *Living on the Level* (Boston: Houghton Mifflin, 1954).

37. "Indoor-Outdoor Living Room," *Architectural Forum* 81 (December 1944): 102.

38. Ethel McCall Head, "Den and Dining—All in One," *Better Homes and Gardens* (January 1947): 89.

4. SLEEPING, HEALTH, AND PRIVACY

1. Alison K. Hoagland, *The Bathroom: A Social History of Cleanliness and The Body* (Santa Barbara, CA: Greenwood Press, 2018); Hoagland, "Introducing the Bathroom: Space and Change in Working-class Houses," *Buildings and Landscapes* 18, no. 2 (Fall 2011): 15–42; Many ideas in this chapter published in Cromley, "Sleeping Around," in *The Banham Lectures*, eds. Jeremy Aynsley and Harriet Atkinson (Oxford and New York: Berg, 2009): 85–99.

2. "The De Leon-Massenet Expeditions," in *Spanish Exploration in the Southwest 1542–1706*, ed. Herbert E. Bolton (repr. Barnes and Noble, 1963), 345–424.

3. On Pear Valley, see E. Chappell and J. Richter," Wealth and Houses in Post-Revolutionary Virginia," in *Perspectives in Vernacular Architecture* 7, eds. Adams and McMurry (Knoxville: Univ. of Tennessee Press, 1997), 5; a corner staircase with angled treads was part of a renovation about 1837.

4. Philip Fithian, *Journal*, Introduction and notes by H. D. Farish, 80.

5. Philip Fithian, *Journal*, 94–95.

6. Kevin M. Sweeney, "Furniture and the Domestic Environment in Wethersfield, Connecticut, 1639–1800," *Connecticut Antiquarian* 36 (1984): 10–39, reprinted in *Material Life*, ed. Robert St. George (1988), 261–90, 281–82; David H. Flaherty, *Privacy in Colonial New England* (Charlottesville: Univ. of Virginia Press, 1972).

7. Kevin M. Sweeney, "Furniture and the Domestic Environment," 286–88. Abbott Lowell Cummings, "Inside the Massachusetts House," in *Com-

mon Places: Readings in American Vernacular Architecture, eds. Upton and Vlach (Athens: Univ. of Georgia Press, 1986), 219–39 traces the activities of different rooms in period houses through the inventories of their contents.

8. Twiss-Garrity, "Getting Comfortable."

9. Richard Cordley, D. D., *Pioneer Days in Kansas* (New York, Boston, and Chicago: Pilgrim Press, 1903), 51.

10. Cordley, *Pioneer Days in Kansas,* 52.

11. Cordley, 101–2.

12. Cordley, 59.

13. Cordley, 59.

14. Christiane Fischer, ed., *Let Them Speak For Themselves—Women in the American West, 1849–1900* (Hamden, CT: The Shoestring Press, 1977), 284–85.

15. Fischer, *Let Them Speak for Themselves,* 286.

16. Fischer, 296.

17. W. E. B. Du Bois, "The Souls of Black Folk," in *Three Negro Classics* (New York: Avon Books, 1965), 256–57.

18. Du Bois, "The Souls of Black Folk," 304. One of these families occupied a house with seven rooms, but only fourteen families out of the fifteen hundred had five rooms or more.

19. Du Bois, 304.

20. Marilyn Thornton Williams, *Washing the Great Unwashed: Public Baths in Urban America, 1840–1920* (Columbus: Ohio State Univ. Press, 1991).

21. John Vlach, *Back of the Big House: The Architecture of Plantation Slavery* (Raleigh: Univ. of North Carolina Press, 1993).

22. David W. Blight, *Frederick Douglass: Prophet of Freedom* (New York: Simon and Schuster, 2018), 55.

23. Miss Eliza Leslie, *The House Book* (Philadelphia: Carey and Hart, 1840), 326, cited in Diethorn, 135.

24. May N. Stone, "The Plumbing Paradox: American Attitudes toward Late Nineteenth-Century Domestic Sanitary Arrangements," *Winterthur Portfolio* 14, no. 3 (Autumn 1979): 283–309. She points out that many middle-class householders did not want the "germ-laden, smelly" toilet inside their clean houses, and preferred to keep on using the privy and chamber pot until bathroom installations were more reliable.

25. "A New Extension Bed," *Scientific American* (Oct. 5, 1898).

26. "A Combined Bed and Sofa," *Scientific American* 74 (June 20, 1896): 390.

27. Boyd Pratt and Christopher Wilson, VAF tour guide to New Mexico.

28. Gervase Wheeler, *Homes for the People in Suburb and Country* (Charles Scribner, 1855; repr. New York: Arno, 1972), 287–89.

29. C. J. Laughlin, "Plantation Architecture in Louisiana," *Architectural Review* 101 (August 1946): 215–21.

30. Louis Henry Gibson, *Convenient Houses, with Fifty Plans for the Housekeeper. Architect and Housewife; a Journey through the House* (New York: T. Y. Crowell, 1889), 158, 161; chapter on one-floor houses shows plans.

31. Alison Kyle Leopold, *Victorian Splendor* (New York: Stewart, Tabori & Chang: Distributed by Workman, 1986), 154–55, chapter: "The Bedroom."

32. Christine Herrick, "First Principles a Department for Young House-keepers," *Woman's Home Companion* (March 1911): 47.

33. Ibid. Christine Herrick assumed that there may still be a wash stand, pitcher, and bowl in the 1910s bedroom and cautioned the house-keeper to cleanse them thoroughly.

34. Sally McMurry, *Families and Farmhouses in Nineteenth-Century America* (New York: Oxford, 1988), 180.

35. Catherine Beecher, *A Treatise on Domestic Economy* (New York: Marsh, Capen Lyon, Webb, 1841; repr. New York: Schocken, 1977), 270

36. Christopher Crowfield [Harriet Beecher Stowe], *House and Home Papers* (Boston: Ticknor and Fields, 1865), 68–69.

37. Christopher Crowfield [Harriet Beecher Stowe], *House and Home Papers* (Boston: Ticknor and Fields, 1865), 68–69.

38. Williams and Jones, "Chapter 7: Bedrooms," *Beautiful Homes* (New York: H.S. Allen, 1885), 84.

39. McMurry, *Families and Farmhouses*, 177–78.

40. Wheeler, *Homes for the People*, 342–3. In eighteenth-century houses the stair hall gained some of its grandeur with large windows on land-ings overlooking the street or garden. But house owners in the nineteenth century, seeking to maximize the number of rooms with fixed functions, walled off these ends of the hall to create hall bedrooms.

41. Herrick, "First Principles," 47.

42. Ann Wentworth, "Modern Bedsteads," *House Beautiful* (Nov. 1911): 185.

43. Cromley, "Masculine/Indian," *Winterthur Portfolio* 31, no. 4 (1996): 265–80.

44. James Jacobs, *Detached America* (Charlottesville: Univ. of Virginia

Press, 2015), 111; he shows 1956 diagrams for expanding the attic into two more bedrooms, from Ryan Homes.

45. Jason Reid, *Get Out of My Room—A History of Teen Bedrooms in America* (Chicago and London: Univ. of Chicago Press, 2017).

46. Zachary Fine, "Letter of Recommendation: Bunk Beds," *New York Times Magazine*, June 19, 2016.

47. National Association of Home Builders.

48. Kate Murphy, "For the Busy Couple, a Bathroom Break," *New York Times*, July 20, 2006.

49. Reid, *Get Out of My Room*, 171–75; teens require privacy for early sexual experimentation.

50. "A Bedroom-Dressing Room Suite," *House Beautiful* (October 1954): 195–98.

51. "It's a Second Living room too," *Better Homes and Gardens* 31 (October 1953): 57–59.

52. *Better Homes and Gardens* (1969).

53. *House and Garden's* Mary Seehafer invited women to give their opinions in a 1982 article.

54. Kate Murphy, "For the Busy Couple."

55. Ibid.

5. CIRCULATION, OR GETTING FROM HERE TO THERE

1. For the circulation of utilities and energy, see Jane Brox, *Brilliant, The Evolution of Artificial Light* (Boston and New York: Houghton Mifflin Harcourt, 2010); David Nye, *Consuming Power: A Social History of American Energies* (Cambridge, MA: MIT Press, 1998); Maureen Ogle, *All the Modern Conveniences: American Household Plumbing, 1840–90* (Baltimore: Johns Hopkins Univ. Press, 1996).

2. "The Development of the American Doorway," *American Architect* 12 (June 1918): 818–23.

3. Fred W. Peterson, *Homes in the Heartland, Balloon Frame Farmhouses of the Upper Midwest, 1850–1920* (Lawrence: Univ. Press of Kansas, 1992), plan p. 79.

4. Cary Carson and Carl Lounsbury, eds., *The Chesapeake House* (Chapel Hill: Univ. of North Carolina Press, 2013). "Bostwick (Bostock) House, Bladensburg, MD, 1746; Drawings and Original Documents" pamphlet (Historic Preservation Program, School of Architecture, Univ. of Maryland, April 2018), 14

5. Michael Ann Williams, "The Little 'Big House': The Use and Meaning of the Single-Pen Dwelling," in *Perspectives in Vernacular Architecture* 2, ed. Camille Wells, 130–36; Dell Upton, "White and Black Landscapes in Eighteenth-Century Virginia," in *Material Life in America, 1600–1800*, ed. Robert Blair St. George (Boston: Northeastern Univ. Press, 1988), 357–69.

6. Mark Wenger, "The Central Passage in Virginia: Evolution of an Eighteenth-Century Living Space," in *Perspectives in Vernacular Architecture* 2, ed. Camille Wells, 137–49.

7. Upton, "White and Black Landscapes," 357–69.

8. *Journal and Letters of Phillip Vickers Fithian* (Williamsburg: Colonial Williamsburg, 1957).

9. Thomas Anburey, *Travels Through the Interior Parts of America* 2, (London, William Lane, 1789) 239, note 20; passages were also used in hot weather for sleeping. See Mark Wenger, "The Central Passage in Virginia," 139.

10. Bainbridge Bunting, *Houses of Boston's Back Bay, an Architectural History 1840–1917* (Cambridge: Harvard Univ. Press, 1967).

11. Kenneth Ames, "Meaning in Artifacts: Hall Furnishings in Victorian America," in *Common Places: Readings in American Vernacular Architecture*, eds. Dell Upton and John Michael Vlach (Athens: Univ. of Georgia Press, 1986): 240–60.

12. Harriette Taber Richardson, "The Inside of the House; the Hall and its Furnishings," *House Beautiful* 41 (Dec. 1916): 38–39.

13. Cromley, *Alone Together: A History of New York's Early Apartments* (Ithaca and London: Cornell Univ. Press, 1990), 14–22.

14. Zachary Violette, "Plans and Priorities," *Buildings and Landscapes* 26 (Fall 2019): 17–42.

15. Cromley, *Alone Together*, 149–56.

16. Charles Eastlake, *Hints on Household Taste in Furnishing, Upholstery and Other Detail* (1878; repr. New York: Dover, 1969), chapter 2.

17. The Gibson House museum in Boston has uncushioned wooden chairs in the reception area to discourage tradesmen from lingering.

18. William Peters, "Interior Decoration," *Inland Architect* 12 (November 1888): 56–57.

19. Mary Gay Humphreys, "City Hallways," *The Decorator and Furnisher* 2 (March 1883); H. R. Pennell, "The City Home . . . Entrance Halls of City Houses," *Indoors and Out* 3 (November 1906): 80–85: "The hall gives the first as well as the final impression of the interior."

20. Michel Foucault, *Discipline and Punish* (New York : Vintage Books, 1995).

21. Frances Glessner diary, February 10, 1907; February 11, 1898 (Manuscripts Collection, Chicago Historical Society); hereafter Glessner diary.

22. Louis Auchincloss, Introduction to Edith Wharton's *Age of Innocence* (New York: Modern Library, 1999), vi–vii.

23. Gillian Flynn, *Sharp Objects* (New York: Random House, 2006).

24. Robert C. Spencer, "The Hall," *The House Beautiful* 24 (Aug. 1908): 49–52, 49.

25. Antoinette Rehmann Perrett, "Our New Houses II—The Living Hall," *Good Housekeeping* 52 (Feb. 1911): 182–87, 182.

26. Perrrett, "Our New Houses II—The Living Hall," 184.

27. Perrett, 182.

28. Martha Cutler, "Desirable Halls," *Harper's Bazar* (Sept. 1910): 544.

29. Ellen Lupton and Abbott Miller, *Kitchens, Bathrooms, and the Aesthetics of Waste* (Cambridge: MIT List Visual Arts Center, 1992), 44.

30. Kingston Heath, *Patina of Place* (Knoxville: Univ. of Tennessee Press, 2001).

6. STORAGE

1. A 1684 pamphlet addressed to readers intending to live in Chesapeake explained how to build a three-room house divided into spaces that reflected English prototypes. It should be eighteen by thirty feet with one partition near the middle; the end space was to be divided into two smaller rooms, which English predecessors had traditionally used for food storage. Many ideas in this chapter first published in Cromley, *Food Axis*.

2. Bacon's Castle inventories taken in 1711 and 1728. Stephenson B. Andrews, ed., "Bacon's Castle," *Research Bulletin for the Preservation of Virginia Antiquities* 3 (1984).

3. Booker T. Washington, *Up from Slavery*, in *Three Negro Classics* (New York: Avon Books, 1965): 29–33.

4. Gustav Stickley, ed., *Craftsman Bungalows* (repr. New York: Dover, 1988), 78–79.

5. Stickley, *Craftsman Bungalows*, 125, 131.

6. "A Well-Arranged Pantry," *Household Conveniences* (New York: Orange Judd Co., 1884), 132.

7. Frank T. Lent, architect, *Sound Sense in Suburban Architecture* (Cranford, NJ: self-published, 1893), 34–35.

8. Cromley, "Frank Lloyd Wright in the Kitchen," *Buildings and Landscapes* 19, no. 1 (Spring 2012): 18–42 passim.

9. Except for homeless people who may wear all the clothing they own at once, having nowhere to store their extra goods.

10. E. C. Hussey, *Home Building* (New York: Leader and Van Hoesen, 1876).

11. Fred W. Peterson, *Homes in the Heartland* (Lawrence: Univ. Press of Kansas, 1992), 83.

12. Downing, "clothes cabinet," *The Architecture of Country Houses* (1850; repr. DaCapo, 1968). A press is a container to hold linens or clothes; it may have hanging space or sliding trays; syn. "closet," *Webster's* 3rd.

13. A. J. Downing, *Villas and Cottages* (New York: Harper, 1857).

14. Henry Urbach, "Closets, Clothes, Disclosure," *Assemblage* 30 (1996): 62–73, 65.

15. Examples of c. 1900 closets in Jan Jennings, *Cheap and Tasteful Dwellings: Design Competitions and the Convenient Interior, 1879–1909* (Knoxville: Univ. of Tennessee Press, 2005): 127.

16. Origins of the wire coat hanger in Wikipedia.

17. Kristina Borrman, "One Standardized House for All—America's Little House," *Buildings and Landscapes* 24, no. 2 (Fall 2017): 37–42.

18. Saulo B. Cwerner, "Clothes at Rest: Elements for a Sociology of the Wardrobe," *Fashion Theory* 5 (March 2001): 80–92, 85–86.

19. E. H. Ries, "Closets Handy and Handsome," *Better Homes and Gardens* (March 1941): 82–83.

20. "An Architect Designs His Own," *House and Garden* (January 1941): 34–35. There is also a small closet beside the fireplace in the living room, perhaps for games, and two more at the entrance to the kitchen, probably for work tools.

21. "Fit your closets to fit your family," *House Beautiful* no. 5 (1941): 77.

22. Shannon Mattern, "Closet Archive," *Places Journal* (July 2017), accessed Aug. 20, 2017, https://doi.org/10.22269/170705. She argues that storage spaces likely contain both nostalgic items with personal meaning and unused objects such as "legacy media"—floppy disks that can no longer be read.

23. Downing, *The Architecture of Country Houses*, design III, symmetrical bracketed cottage, 82; illustration and plan, 85–86.

24. Saulo B. Cwerner, "Clothes at Rest: Elements for a Sociology of the Wardrobe," *Fashion Theory* 5 (March 2001): 80–92, 87–88.

25. Henry Urbach, "Closets, Clothes, Disclosure," *Assemblage* 30 (1996): 62–73.

26. Joy Williams, "Owning It," in *The Visiting Privilege: New and Collected Stories* (Vintage, 2016; repr. in *New York Times Magazine*, Nov. 12, 2017), 106.

FOR FURTHER READING

Alexander, Christopher, and Sara Ishikawa, Murray Silverstein, with Max Jacobson, Ingrid Fiksdahl-King, and Shlomo Angel. *A Pattern Language: Towns, Buildings, Construction*. New York: Oxford Univ. Press, 1977.

Ames, Kenneth L. *Death in the Dining Room and Other Tales of Victorian Culture*. Philadelphia: Temple Univ. Press, 1992.

Andrzejewski, Anna Vemer. *Building Power: Architecture and Surveillance in Victorian America*. Knoxville: Univ. of Tennessee Press, 2008.

Barile, Kerri S., and Jamie C. Brandon, eds. *Household Chores and Household Choices: Theorizing the Domestic Sphere in Historical Archaeology*. Tuscaloosa: Univ. of Alabama Press, 2004.

Beecher, Catherine E. *Treatise on Domestic Economy*. New York: Harper and Brothers, 1845.

Beecher, Catherine E., and Harriet Beecher Stowe. *American Woman's Home*. Hartford:, CT, Harriet Beecher Stowe Center, 1864; repr. New Brunswick:, NJ, Rutgers Univ. Press, 2002.

Benjamin, Asher. *The American Builder's Companion*. 6th ed. 1827; repr. New York: Dover, 1969.

Bishir, Catherine. "Jacob Holt: An American Builder." In *Common Places: Readings in American Vernacular Architecture*, 447–81.

———. *The Bellamy Mansion, Wilmington, NC*. Raleigh: Historic Preservation Foundation of North Carolina, 2004.

Bishir, Catherine, Charlotte V. Brown, Carl R. Lounsbury, and Ernest H. Wood III. *Architects and Builders in North Carolina: A History of the Practice of Building*. Chapel Hill: Univ. of North Carolina Press, 1990.

Blumenson, J. *Identifying American Architecture: A Pictorial Guide to Styles and Terms*. Nashville: American Association for State and Local History, 1977.

Bok, Edward W. "Abolish the Dining Room." *Collier's* 79 (January 15, 1927): 10.

Brox, Jane. *Brilliant, The Evolution of Artificial Light*. Boston and New York: Houghton Mifflin Harcourt, 2010.

Buchanan, Paul. *Stratford Hall and Other Architectural Studies*. Stratford, VA: Robert E. Lee Memorial Association, Inc., 1998.

Buildings and Landscapes, formerly titled *Perspectives in Vernacular Archi-tecture*, is a periodic volume with articles based on significant research on Vernacular Architecture topics. Contents are diverse and wide-rang-ing, covering national and international locations, time periods from the seventeenth century to the present, methods, and theories.

Bushman, Richard. *The Refinement of America: Persons, Houses, Cities.* New York: Vintage, 1993.

Carson, Barbara. *Ambitious Appetites: Dining Behavior and Patterns of Consumption in Federal Washington.* Washington, DC: The American Institute of Architects Press, 1990.

Carson, Cary, Ronald Hoffman, and Peter J. Albert, eds. *Of Consuming Interests: The Style of Life in the Eighteenth Century.* Charlottesville and London: United States Capitol Historical Society and Univ. Press of Virginia, 1994.

Carter, Thomas. *Building Zion: The Material World of Mormon Settlement.* Minneapolis: Univ. of Minnesota Press, 2015.

——, ed. *Images of an American Land: Vernacular Architecture in the United States.* Albuquerque: Univ. of New Mexico Press, 1997.

Carter, Thomas, and Elizabeth Cromley. *Invitation to Vernacular Architec-ture.* Knoxville: Univ. of Tennessee Press, 2005.

Carter, Thomas, and Peter L. Goss. *Utah's Historic Architecture: A Guide.* Salt Lake City: Univ. of Utah Press, 1986.

Chappell, Edward, and Julie Richter. "Wealth and Houses in Post-Revo-lutionary Virginia." In *Exploring Everyday Landscapes: Perspectives in Vernacular Architecture 7*, edited by Annmarie Adams and Sally McMurry, 3–22. Knoxville: Univ. of Tennessee Press, 1997.

Chow, Renee. *Suburban Space: The Fabric of Dwelling.* Berkeley: Univ. of California Press, 2002.

Clark, Clifford. *The American Family Home.* Chapel Hill: Univ. of North Carolina Press, 1986.

Cohen, Lizabeth A. "Embellishing a Life of Labor: An Interpretation of the Material Culture of American Working-Class Homes, 1885–1915." In *Common Places*, 261–81.

Cowan, Ruth. *More Work for Mother: The Ironies of Household Technology from the Open Hearth to the Microwave.* New York: Basic, 1983.

Cromley, Elizabeth C. *The Food Axis: Cooking, Eating, and the Architecture of American Houses.* Charlottesville and London: Univ. of Virginia Press, 2010.

———. "Sleeping Around: A History of American Beds and Bedrooms." In *The Banham Lectures: Essays on Designing the Future*, edited by Jeremy Aynsley and Harriet Atkinson. Oxford and New York: Berg, 2009.

———. *Alone Together: A History of New York's Early Apartments*. Ithaca: Cornell Univ. Press, 1990.

Cummings, Abbott Lowell. *The Framed Houses of Massachusetts Bay, 1625–1725*. Cambridge: Harvard Univ. Press, 1979.

Dolkart, Andrew Scott. *Biography of a Tenement House in New York City*. Charlottesville and London: Univ. of Virginia Press, 2010.

Ellis, Clifton, and Rebecca Ginsburg. *Cabin, Quarter, Plantation: Architecture and Landscapes of North American Slavery*. New Haven: Yale Univ. Press, 2010.

Flore, Fredie, and Cammie McAtee, eds. *The Politics of Furniture: Identity, Diplomacy, and Persuasion in Post-War Interiors*. New York: Routledge, 2017.

Foley, Mary M. *The American House*. New York: Harper, 1980.

Foucault, Michel. *Discipline and Punish: The Birth of the Prison*. New York: Vintage Books, 1995.

Foy, Jessica H., and Karal Ann Marling. *The Arts and the American Home, 1890–1930*. Knoxville: Univ. of Tennessee Press, 1994.

Foy, Jessica H., and Thomas Schlereth, eds. *American Home Life, 1880–1930: A Social History of Spaces and Services*. Knoxville: Univ. of Tennessee Press, 1992.

Franck, Karen A., and Sherry Ahrentzen, eds. *New Households, New Housing*. New York: Van Nostrand Reinhold, 1989.

Garrison, J. Ritchie. *Landscape and Material Life in Franklin County, Massachusetts, 1770–1860*. Knoxville: Univ. of Tennessee Press, 1991.

———. *Two Carpenters: Architecture and Building in Early New England, 1799–1859*. Knoxville: Univ. of Tennessee Press, 2006.

Gibson, Louis Henry. *Convenient Houses, with Fifty Plans for the Housekeeper, Architect and Housewife; a Journey through the House*. 1854. Reprint, New York, T. Y. Crowell & co. [1889].

Glassie, Henry. *Folk Housing in Middle Virginia: A Structural Analysis of Historic Artifacts*. Knoxville Univ. of Tennessee Press, 1975.

Glessner, Frances. *Diary*. Manuscripts Collection, Chicago Historical Society. Feb. 11, 1898 to Feb. 10, 1907.

Gowans, Alan. *Styles and Types of North American Architecture: Social Function and Cultural Expression*. New York: HarperCollins, 1992.

Groth, Paul. *Living Downtown: The History of Residential Hotels in the United States*. Berkeley: Univ. of California Press, 1994.

Grover, Kathryn, ed. *Dining in America, 1850–1900*. Amherst: Univ. of Massachusetts Press, 1987.

Handlin, David P. *The American Home: Architecture and Society, 1815–1915*. Boston: Little Brown, 1979.

Hayden, Dolores. *The Grand Domestic Revolution: A History of Feminist Designs for American Homes, Neighborhoods, and Cities*. Cambridge: MIT Press, 1981.

———. *Building Suburbia: Green Fields and Urban Growth*. New York: Pantheon Books, 2003.

Hayward, Mary Ellen. *Baltimore's Alley Houses: Homes for Working People since the 1780s*. Baltimore: Johns Hopkins Univ. Press, 2008.

Heath, Kingston. *The Patina of Place: Cultural Weathering of a New England Industrial Landscape*. Knoxville: Univ. of Tennessee Press, 2001.

Herman, Bernard. *Town House: Architecture and Material Life in the Early American City, 1780–1830*. Chapel Hill: Univ. of North Carolina Press, 2005.

———. *Architecture and Rural Life in Central Delaware, 1700–1900*. Knoxville Univ. of Tennessee Press, 1987.

Hubka, Thomas C. "The New England Farmhouse Ell: Fact and Symbol of Nineteenth Century Farm Improvement." In *Perspectives in Vernacular Architecture 2*, edited by Camille Wells. Columbia: Univ. of Missouri Press, 1986.

———. *Big House, Little House, Back House, Barn: The Connected Farm Buildings of New England*. Hanover, NH: Univ. Press of New England, 1984.

———. *Houses without Names: Architectural Nomenclature and the Classification of America's Common Houses*. Knoxville: Univ. of Tennessee Press, 2013.

Ierley, Merritt. *The Comforts of Home: The American House and the Evolution of Modern Convenience*. New York: Clarkson Potter, 1999.

Jennings, Jan. *Cheap and Tasteful Dwellings: Design Competitions and the Convenient Interior, 1879–1909*. Knoxville: Univ. of Tennessee Press, 2005.

Jones, Robert T., ed. *Authentic Small Houses of the Twenties*. New York: Dover Publications, 1987; reprint of 1929 original.

King, Anthony D. *The Bungalow: The Production of a Global Culture*. New York: Oxford Univ. Press, 1995.

Klimasmith, Betsy. *At Home in the City: Urban Domesticity in American Literature and Culture, 1850–1930*. Durham: Univ. of New Hampshire Press, 2005.

Lane, Barbara Miller. *Housing and Dwelling: Perspectives on Modern Domestic Architecture*. London and New York: Routledge, 2007.

Lanier, Gabrielle, and Bernard Herman. *Everyday Architecture of the Mid-Atlantic*. Baltimore: Johns Hopkins Univ. Press, 1997.

Loeb, Carolyn. *Entrepreneurial Vernacular: Developers' Subdivisions in the 1920s*. Baltimore: Johns Hopkins Univ. Press, 2019.

Lounsbury Carl R., ed. *The Material World of Eyre Hall: Four Centuries of Chesapeake History*. Baltimore: Maryland Center for History and Culture in association with D. Giles Limited, 2021.

Lupkin, Paula, and Penny Sparke. *Shaping the American Interior: Structures, Contexts, and Practices*. New York: Routledge, 2018.

Lupton, Ellen, and Abbott Miller. *Kitchens, Bathrooms, and the Aesthetics of Waste*. Cambridge: MIT List Visual Arts Center, 1992.

Martin, Charles E. *Hollybush: Folk Building and Social Change in an Appalachian Community*. Knoxville: Univ. of Tennessee Press, 1984.

McAlester, Virginia and Lee. *A Field Guide to American Houses*. New York: Alfred Knopf, 2000.

McMurray, Sally. *Families and Farmhouses in Nineteenth-Century America*. New York: Oxford Univ. Press, 1988.

McMurray, Sally, and Nancy Van Dolsen. *Architecture and Landscape of the Pennsylvania Germans, 1720–1920*. Philadelphia: Univ. of Pennsylvania Press, 2011.

Nye, David. *Consuming Power: A Social History of American Energies*. Cambridge: MIT Press, 1998.

Ogle, Maureen. *All the Modern Conveniences: American Household Plumbing, 1840–90*. Baltimore: Johns Hopkins Univ. Press, 1996.

Olmert, Michael. *Kitchens, Smoke Houses, and Privies: Outbuildings and the Architecture of Daily Life in the Eighteenth-Century Mid-Atlantic*. Ithaca: Cornell Univ. Press, 2009.

Peterson, Fred. *Homes in the Heartland: Balloon Frame Farmhouses of the Upper Midwest, 1850–1920*. Lawrence: Univ. Press of Kansas, 1992.

Plunz, Richard. *A History of Housing In New York City*. New York: Columbia Univ. Press, 1990.

Pocius, Gerald L. *A Place to Belong: Community Order and Everyday Space in Calvert, Newfoundland*. Athens: Univ. of Georgia Press, 1991.

Reed, Roger, and Greer Hardwicke. *Carriage House to Auto House*. Brookline: Brookline Preservation Commission, 2002.

Reid, Jason. *Get Out of My Room: A History of Teen Bedrooms in America*. Chicago and London: Univ. of Chicago Press, 2017.

Reiff, Daniel D. *Houses from Books: Treatises, Pattern Books, and Catalogs in American Architecture, 1738–1950: A History and Guide*. Univ. Park: The Pennsylvania State Univ. Press, 2000.

Rideout, Orlando, V. *Building the Octagon*. Washington, DC: American Institute of Architects Press, 1989.

Rifkind, Carol. *A Field Guide to American Architecture*. New York: New American Library, 1980.

Seale, William. *The Tasteful Interlude: American Interiors through the Camera's Eye, 1860–1917*. 2d ed. Nashville, TN: American Association for State and Local History, 1981.

Simpson, Pamela H. *Cheap, Quick, and Easy: Imitative Architectural Materials, 1870–1930*. Knoxville: Univ. of Tennessee Press, 1999.

Small, Nora Pat. "New England Farmhouses in the Early Republic: Rhetoric and Reality," in *Shaping Communities, Perspectives in Vernacular Architecture 6*, edited by Hudgins and Cromley, 33–45. Knoxville: Univ. of Tennessee Press, 1997.

Smith, Oliver P. *Victorian Domestic Architect: A Facsimile of Oliver P. Smith's [1854]* The Domestic Architect. Watkins Glen, NY: American Life Foundation, 1978.

Stevenson, Katherine Cole, and H. Ward Jandl. *Houses by Mail: A Guide to Houses from the Sears, Roebuck and Company*. Washington, DC: Preservation Press, 1986.

Stickley, Gustav, ed. *Craftsman Bungalows*. Reprint, New York: Dover, 1988.

Teegan, Otto. "Houses in Our Towns of Tomorrow." *The Arts and Decoration Book of Successful Houses*. New York: Robert M. McBride and Co., 1940.

Tolbert, Lisa. *Constructing Townscapes: Space and Society in Antebellum Tennessee*. Chapel Hill: Univ. of North Carolina Press, 1999.

Ulrich, Laurel Thatcher. *The Age of Homespun: Objects and Stories in the Creation of an American Myth*. New York: Vintage, 2001.

Upton, Dell. "Pattern Books and Professionalism: Aspects of the Transformation of Domestic Architecture in America, 1800–1860." *Winterthur Portfolio* 19 (Summer/Autumn 1984): 107–50.

——. "White and Black Landscapes in Eighteenth-Century Virginia." In *Material Life in America, 1600–1800*, edited by Robert Blair St. George, 357–69. Boston: Northeastern Univ. Press, 1988.

Upton, Dell, and John Vlach, eds. *Common Places: Readings in American Vernacular Architecture.* Athens: Univ. of Georgia Press, 1986.

Violette, Zachary. "Plans and Priorities, Multifamily Housing Types and French-Canadian Builders in Northern New England, 1890–1950." *Buildings and Landscapes* 26 (Fall 2019): 17-42.

Vlach, John. *Back of the Big House: The Architecture of Plantation Slavery.* Raleigh: Univ. of North Carolina Press, 1993.

Walker, Lester. *American Shelter: An Illustrated Encyclopedia of the American Home.* Woodstock, NY: Overlook Press, 1981.

Warner, Sam Bass. *Street-Car Suburbs: The Process of Growth in Boston.* Cambridge: Harvard Univ. Press, 1962.

Washington, Booker T. *Up from Slavery.* Oxford and New York: Oxford Univ. Press, 1995.

Wells, Camille. *Material Witnesses: Domestic Architecture and Plantation Landscapes in Early Virginia.* Charlottesville and London: 2018.

Wenger, Mark. "The Dining Room in Early Virginia." In *Perspectives in Vernacular Architecture* 3, edited by Herman and Carter, 149–59.

Wheeler, Gervase. *Rural Homes or Sketches of Houses Suited to American Country Life.* New York: Scribner, 1851.

Williams, Michael Ann. *Homeplace: The Social Use and Meaning of the Folk Dwelling in Southwestern North Carolina.* Charlottesville: Univ. of Virginia Press, 2004.

Wilson, Chris. *The Myth of Santa Fe: Creating a Modern Regional Tradition.* Albuquerque: Univ. of New Mexico Press, 1997.

Wright, Gwendolyn. *Building the Dream: A Social History of Housing in America.* New York: Pantheon Books, 1981.

——. *Moralism and the Model Home: Domestic Architecture and Cultural Conflict in Chicago.* Chicago: Univ. of Chicago Press, 1980.

INDEX

Page numbers in **boldface** refer to illustrations.

backhouse, 9

bakehouse, 9

Balderston, Lydia Ray, 22

basement kitchens, 13–15

bathing: in nineteenth century, 82; with pitcher and basin, 82, **83;** portable bathtub, 82, **83**

bathrooms, 99–103; three-fixture bathroom, **86,** 87

bed types and special bedroom furniture, 73, **81,** 87, **88,** 98

bedrooms, 71–103; ethnic variations, 89, **90, 91, 91;** location in house, 74–76, **75, 77,** 92; multi-purpose, 99–102; and privacy 89, 91; in seventeenth century, 72; in tenements, 80

Bevier, Isabel, **21,** 122

Bungalow, 125–26

buttery, 6

chamber pots and privies, 79–84, **84, 85, 86**

children's bedrooms, 95, 97–98; and gender, 98

circulation, 105–27; definition, 105–6; dining room as 124, **125;** economical 110, 123–26; kitchen as circulation hub, **123,** 124; in open plan, 126–27; as site for ornament 106–8; status of users, 105–6, 108–12

closets for clothes: 138–47; eighteenth-century, 139–40; gender in, 144–45, **144;** location of 140–47; nineteenth-century, **140,** 140–43; size of, **143,** 144–45; twentieth century, 144–47, **144**

cooking, 1–29; in apartments, 60–61; in cookstoves, 15–16, **16, 17, 24;** fireplace, 1, 4–6, 15, 30; in a kettle, **9, 10;** with new technologies 12, **13;** on raised hearth, 5–6; in rural houses, 23, **24**

dairy: freestanding dairy, **6;** milkroom or milkhouse, **5;** storing dairy products, 2, 6–7, 131

dining room, 51, 58; built-in, 61–62, **62, 63;** first dining room, 52–53; naming 53–55; storage, 61–67, **64, 66,** 133–34, **134**

—eighteenth century, **53,** 55, 69; as largest room, 54; ornamental storage, 133–34, **134;** as a sitting room, 55

—nineteenth century, 56–61, **58, 59;** as circulation, 124–25, **125;** nature in, 56–58, **57;** in rural houses, 58–59

—twentieth century, 61–67; merging with kitchen, 57, 62, **64, 66,** 154; merging with living room, 62, **63,** 65, 68; elimination of, 61–62, 68

dining-room additions, **53,** 54, 66

doors, 106–9; **106, 107, 108, 109, 110;** into living room, 120–22, 125

Downing, A. J., 141

eating spaces, 51–52, 59; in kitchen, 57, **64**

Edbrooke and Burnham, 38

electricity, **26,** 27

"ell" additions, 9, 12, 15, 151

Fithian, Philip, diary, 55, 112

food storage: beneath the floor, 133; in cellar, 25; in cool water, **131;** in dedicated rooms, **6, 7,** 130; in outbuildings, **6;** in seventeenth century, 2, 129–30

garage, 109, **148,** 148–49

hall, 105–27, 111–17; eighteenth century, 72; nineteenth century, 113–19, **117;** twentieth century, 120

hall stand, **114,** 114–15

health, in bedrooms, 93–95; fresh air, **95;** healthiest beds, 93–95; unhealthy beds, **94**

home economics: defined, 19; goals of, 19; influences on kitchen design, 21–22, 137

Hood, Raymond, 67

Hussey, E. C., 141

Keene, E. S., **27**

kitchens, 1–30; in cellars, 13–15, **14;** as circulation hub, 124; consolidation, 21; migrating, 9–11, **11;** as outbuildings, **3,** 4; second or third, 28–30; storage in, 28, 135–38, **135, 138;** unified cabinetry, **28,** 137–38, **138**

Lakey, Charles, 37

Landefeld and Hatch, 67

lean-to additions, 4, 151

Lent, Frank, 19, **20**

living room, 39–44, **39, 42, 43**–44, 122, 153

living-kitchen, 45, **46,** 47, **49, 68,** 69, **126**

master suite, 99–100

multi-family dwelling: cooking smells, **17,** 17; dining rooms, **58,** 59–60; kitchenless, 60, **60;** living rooms, 48; planning a unit, 17; sleeping spaces, 79–83, **92**

nurseries, 19, 95–97, **96,** 153

one-room house, 31–32, **32,** 72, 151

outbuildings, 2, 4, 7–8, **33,** 34

pantry, **21;** butler's pantry, **20;** cabinetry, 136–37; as circulation path, 122, **123, 135,** 135; function, 19–20 parlor, 31, 34, **41,** 153

Pond, Irving and Allen, 37

preserving food, 19; canning, 25; ethnic variations, 29–30; in freezer, 133; in root-cellar, **8;** in smokehouse, 4, 132

privacy, 77, **78,** 87, 116–17; 122, 126–27, 154–55

Raeder, Coffin and Crocker, 38

recreation room, 44–5, **45**

refrigerator, 22, **22, 26,** 27, **132,** 132–33

Richardson, H. H., **132**

room names: in modern houses, 43; Mrs. Glessner's, 38; nineteenth-century alternatives to "parlor,"36–37, **37;** specifying function, 2; in tenements, 17, **39**

root cellar, **8,** 8, 130

row-houses, parlors, 34–36, **35, 36;** bedrooms, 89–90; circulation, 113–15

sleeping, 71–72, 151; for the enslaved, 3, 8, 80–81, **81;** in the kitchen, 18, 79; for middle class, 87, 152; in parlor, 43; porch, **75;** in rural houses, 76–78; for servants, **81,** 81–82, 152

smokehouse, 131–32

social rooms. *See* living room, parlor, recreation room

social-room materials, 49–50

stairs, 97, 112, 114, 117–19; for servants, 113–14, **112, 113, 117;** for surveillance, 105, 119–20, **119;** in tenements, **116**. *See also* hall

storage, 129–49; on porches and balconies, 148; and sleeping spaces, 76; in yard, 147, **147**

—in dining rooms: in built-in furniture, 36, **36, 63**

—in kitchens: cabinet opening to both dining room and kitchen, 134; cabinets above and below counters, 28, **28,** 135; special storage rooms, **135**

summer kitchen, 16

tenements, 17, **39, 116**

Treat and Folz, 38

two-room house, 32, 33, 72, 74

Vaux, Calvert, 141–42, **142**

water supply: to bathroom, 8; external pump, 6; to houses, 25–27, 85, 155; to kitchen, **17,** 25

White, Charles E., **63**

Whitehouse, Francis, **37,** 38

Wright, Frank Lloyd, 65, 137